Praise for C

Jeffery Leininger's book gives us a glimpse into the heart of someone who cares deeply about the callings God gives to His own. Leininger has every reader in mind as he engages us with great Christians who lived their callings, especially when it was not easy. You will love the stories and the rich substance. You will meet new people and learn new things—I did! As I read this book, I reflected on my own journey and how God was at work even when I did not know it. Be ready to think and rethink your life and callings. In a day when we "sugarcoat" too much of life, afraid of struggle and challenge, Leininger reminds us we have a high and holy calling in Christ for His purpose. After reading the book, I found myself in Hebrews 11, especially verse 38, as one of those "of whom the world was not worthy." You and I are not called by the world, but by Jesus. Happy and thoughtful reading!

REV. DR. ALLAN R. BUSS
LCMS NORTHERN ILLINOIS DISTRICT PRESIDENT

Many books deserve to be read. A precious few merit being reread over and over. This is one of them. Pastor Leininger's insights in identifying the various manifestations of our vocation-related temptations are both wise and much needed. This is an important book. I wish I had read it several years ago. It would have spared me the misery of learning so many of its lessons the hard way!

REV. SCOTT CHRISTENSON
SENIOR PASTOR
ST. PAUL'S LUTHERAN CHURCH
AND SCHOOL, ORANGE, CA

This book is a wonderful, accessible exposition of Luther's doctrine of vocation, and it deserves a place in every college, congregation, and home library. Although it is written for college students, I believe every Christian would benefit from reading this encouraging and thought-provoking text. The narrative examples are particularly helpful, and the discussion questions make this suitable for group Bible study as well as a classroom setting. All Christians struggle at some point with the big question of how to discern God's will for their lives. This book firmly reminds us that God is in control and it is He who gifts us with our callings in all aspects of our daily life.

DEACONESS DR. CYNTHIA LUMLEY
WESTFIELD HOUSE OF THEOLOGICAL STUDIES, CAMBRIDGE

Dr. Leininger's *Callings for Life* demonstrates that all people have a place in the kingdom of God on both sides of heaven. Leininger outlines that, on this side of heaven, we have many callings in life—some we are prepared for and others wholly unprepared; some callings that bring great joy and others great heartache. Dr. Leininger juxtaposes the greatest authors of the Christian faith and the greatest Biblical characters of all time over and against the everyday person living in this time, with these problems, and with these particular thoughts and questions on their callings. Leininger's work is brilliant, encouraging the reader to focus on our callings within our families, communities, and the places in which we learn, as we look toward our future callings in life that God reveals in His own time. Leininger also reminds us of our ultimate calling—the calling of life after death with Jesus. This is won for us in by Christ in victory as He declared death to be dead, calling us from darkness into His marvelous light. Leininger prepares us to face the callings of today until God calls us home to be with Him.

REV. GERARD I. BOLLING
ASSOCIATE PASTOR
BETHLEHEM LUTHERAN CHURCH, ST. LOUIS, MO

Dr. Jeffrey Leininger makes a welcome contribution to understanding God's purpose for one's life. Strongly grounded in Scripture and Luther's writings on vocation, Dr. Leininger's book develops contemporary applications that will enlighten and inspire a wide range of readers. I particularly appreciate his focus on recognizing the vocations God has given us in the present, ordinary circumstances of our daily lives.

MARILYN REINECK
VICE PRESIDENT OF ACADEMIC AFFAIRS
CONCORDIA UNIVERSITY, ST. PAUL

The journey of life is far from a clear path along a clean pathway. That's why we need the Holy Spirit and God-sent guides. For decades, Jeff Leininger has been engaging young adults with an empathic ear. There's something we all can learn from his learnings. Fastened to his stout academic credentials, this useful volume provides us with practical wisdom and spiritual winsomeness. Leininger presents examples from Rosa Young to Martin Luther, from Dietrich Bonhoeffer to Gudina Tumsa, making plain that the Light of the World works His saving plan within the everyday purposes of all of us.

REV. DR. JOHN A. NUNES
PRESIDENT
CONCORDIA COLLEGE NEW YORK

Callings for
LIFE

God's Plan, Your Purpose

JEFFREY LEININGER

CONCORDIA PUBLISHING HOUSE · SAINT LOUIS

For our children, Gracie and Andy,
whose love has brought this earthly father a heavenly joy.

Published by Concordia Publishing House
3558 S. Jefferson Ave., St. Louis, MO 63118-3968
1-800-325-3040 • cph.org

Manufactured in the United States of America

Library of Congress Cataloging-in-Publication Data

Names: Leininger, Jeffrey, author.
Title: God's plan for your life : callings, vocations, and the reason you were born / Jeffrey Leininger.
Description: Saint Louis, MO : Concordia Publishing House, 2020. | Summary:
    "College students and recent graduates are often uncertain about the
    future, wondering if they chose the right path and will land a job.
    Adults in stable jobs and full-time parents often experience feelings of
    being stuck, frustrated, or unhappy; they think the grass is always
    greener on the other side of the fence. Those who have lost their jobs
    or are retired may wonder what the future holds and if they will be able
    to support themselves"-- Provided by publisher.
Identifiers: LCCN 2020022109 (print) | LCCN 2020022110 (ebook) | ISBN
    9780758666314 (paperback) | ISBN 9780758666321 (ebook)
Subjects: LCSH: Vocation--Christianity.
Classification: LCC BV4740 .L45 2020 (print) | LCC BV4740 (ebook) | DDC 248.4--dc23
LC record available at https://lccn.loc.gov/2020022109
LC ebook record available at https://lccn.loc.gov/2020022110

2   3   4   5   6   7   8   9   10   29   28   27   26   25   24   23   22   21

CONTENTS

FOREWORD

I had completed a full draft of the entirety of this book, and then a worldwide pandemic raged across the globe. It has now infected millions, killed tens of thousands, brought economic activity to a standstill, and placed upon all our lives an unsettled pause. As I write this foreword, much remains uncertain and out of focus. Many people are questioning much of what they once found firm and foundational. We live in a new world now, where we try on our old assumptions only to quickly cast them off like the faded fashions of a different age.

It is then, perhaps, the greatest endorsement of this book that, rather than its message now feeling out of place or irrelevant, it has taken on new energy and importance. More than ever we must strive to hear the voice of God, discern His calling upon our lives, and seek His will and purposes in every trial and circumstance. COVID-19 has not made this book irrelevant; it has made it more urgent.

My prayer is that the reader will be edified by a challenging but transformative understanding of the nature of our callings from God. Martin Luther's sixteenth-century insights on vocation have refreshed relevance today, as we wrestle with greater questions about purpose, love, service, and sacrifice.

Although gleaned from over two decades of pastoral experience, the narrative examples found in this book are fictional. Any connection between the names of the characters and any actual people or particular situations is purely accidental.

May God richly bless you through these words, and may this message convict and comfort, educate and edify you in your callings for life.

CHAPTER 1

CALLINGS

*Our calling in life is better understood in
the plural rather than the singular.*

· ·

THE MYTH OF THE ONE GREAT THING

It's out there, if I can only discover it. . . . It's
sent to me from God, if I can only discern it. . . .
It's world-changing, if I can only accomplish it.
. . . It's the one great thing I'm set on this earth
to do, and only by seeking after it will I find
true fulfillment.

· ·

I n these and in so many other ways, we convince ourselves that
we have one great calling in life—a singular, spiritual, seismic,
holy, and otherworldly task that the Almighty has created, even
preordained for us to accomplish. But this is a myth—a confusing
and often destructive one at that. We are indeed all called by God
through the Gospel, redeemed by the blood of Christ, baptized into
His family of faith, and given purpose and meaning. This is all true in
our primary calling as baptized children of God. But nowhere do the
Scriptures reveal one great thing we are meant to accomplish in this
life. God has not said that each individual person is given a single,

1

dramatic, earthshaking task to achieve in order to fulfill his or her purpose on earth. That is to say, *our calling in life is better understood in the plural rather than the singular.* We should be speaking of calling*s* rather than calling. Because of the freedom we have in Christ Jesus, God has placed us in multiple calling*s* in this world and gifted us to be His instruments in multiple ways to a world in need.

The myth of the "one great thing" is disseminated through popular culture, academia, and even in well-meaning Christian circles. A simple Google search of the question "How do I find my purpose?" results in dozens of books, websites, checklists, and seminars promising to help you find the ONE THING, and thus bring clarity and vision to your life. It might take the form of the most fulfilling job—because the drudgery of your current work is certainly not what you're called to do! It might take the form of a specific person—as if finding "*the one*" is the *one* thing that will finally bring meaning to your life. It might even be something more noble—a great charitable work or a life-changing nonprofit established to alleviate suffering in the world. Any of these things might be valuable and important, but the popular myth fools us into thinking that unless we find the singular purpose we were born for, our lives will be miserable, meandering, and meaningless.

In academia, the concept of vocation (from *vocatio*: Latin for "calling") has become immensely popular, especially at Christian universities. Often it's a way of inspiring students to seek that one great purpose God has given them, which, when discovered in college (perhaps "revealed" to them in a challenging class with an inspiring professor), will lead them to change the world. Universities within the Protestant tradition will baptize the quest for the one great thing by using the term *vocation* because of its historical connection to the Reformation and its broad application to every student. Even secular schools offer courses to help students discover their purpose in life.

Well-meaning Christian authors and pastors seek to aid and inspire the sheep under their care through books, sermon series, and seminars on sanctified decision-making or discerning God's will for your life.

Peruse any Christian bookstore, and you'll find dozens of items for purchase with this type of language: "God's purpose for you," "God's will," "hearing God's voice," "knowing God's direction," "discovering God's will," "purpose for your life"—or some combination thereof.

There is value in all of this, of course. People need focus and direction. It's good to be inspired about what God has in store for us. Many people "discover" themselves in college and are led to do remarkable things in the world. A Christian university should support students' spiritual discernment about their future. It is wholesome and even necessary to seek God's will in making important decisions, such as whom I should marry, where I should live, what type of work I should do, or how I can make a lasting impact.

The myth of the "one great," however, underlies many of these approaches. The problem is that we too often think in the singular rather than the plural: *calling* rather than *callings*. The urgency to discover and discern God's singular, sacred, seismic purpose constantly harasses us; we're afraid that if we miss out our lives will disintegrate into a fog of confusion and purposelessness.

Neglect and Regret

Scott became a Christian later in life. Although he was raised in a good, loving home, his parents never wanted to push religion on him, thinking it would be better for him to make this decision on his own. His life was not miserable or out of control, but he describes it as having a pall over it—an overlying darkness or heaviness from which he could temporarily distract himself but which could never be completely lifted. Introduced to Jesus in college, through Christian fellowship and the work of the Spirit in the Word, Scott came to understand the forgiveness given at the cross and the promise of eternal life at the empty tomb. The pall was lifted, and after he was baptized, Scott said that a lightness and brightness replaced the dark heaviness of a life lived without God.

With this new knowledge of Christ Jesus, Scott's life continued down a path of blessings and accomplishments. He graduated *magna cum laude*; made a good career choice; has a wonderful wife and three smart, talented, and well-adjusted children; has enjoyed advancement at work; and has a nice home (with a manageable mortgage). But ever since his conversion, Scott became increasingly fascinated with what to do with his newfound life in Christ. *Surely there must be something more,* he thought. *What amazing thing does God want me to do with my life now that I've given it over to Him?* To not discover the single, central purpose for which God had saved him seemed to him like a waste of the salvation he'd been given. Scott had fallen prey to the myth of the one great thing.

Scott grew increasingly neglectful of his day-to-day responsibilities and relationships. His work at a secular company seemed like a worldly waste of time and energy. He read book after book that promised to unleash inner spiritual potential. Instead of going to soccer games or helping with homework, he took every opportunity to attend religious retreats or escape to seminars about discovering God's hidden purpose for him. He eventually quit serving on the church council—the drudgery of budgets, performance reviews, and raising money for a new roof couldn't possibly compete with the excitement of what God would call him to do. Even his marriage began to suffer. The hard work and perseverance required to sustain a relationship amid the piles of dirty dishes and dirty laundry seemed less attractive and exciting than the pursuit of this one, true, dramatic calling that God would reveal to him . . . eventually, if he just kept seeking. His wife grew understandably more hurt and resentful as Scott's self-imposed sanctified quest for meaning became more important than a renewal of love, affection, and energy toward her. They grew further apart and emotionally isolated from each other, all while living under one roof and giving the pretense of a successful Christian marriage. A fractured home, a messy divorce, further isolation . . . and Scott's still searching.

Scott's life is Exhibit A in how an obsession with the one great thing results in a sinful neglect of the many worthy callings God gives. His dismissive attitude toward the seemingly mundane tasks of home, work, congregation, and community stemmed from a quest to discover God's singular central purpose for him—a quest more enticing the more elusive it became. If only he could have thought in the plural rather than the singular and embraced a life full of varied but worthy callings, rather than a singular calling. Scott could have avoided the tragedy of a life in pursuit of the illusory one great thing in careless neglect of the many great things already present.

Exhibit B: Sarah was meant for more. Since grade school at St. Mark's Lutheran and all throughout high school, Sarah's teachers regarded her as one of the best and brightest. Talented, smart, hardworking, and driven, even her friends' parents knew she was destined for greatness. At the small, Christian college she attended, Sarah was involved in *everything*: sports, music, mission trips, student council, and the chapel worship team. Her selection to homecoming court senior year meant more than a popularity contest: Sarah's friends and classmates saw Christ shining through her, knowing that her many gifts would be put to good use in God's kingdom.

Fast-forward twenty years. Sarah is frequently moody and some-times even depressed. Her life is great, on the one hand. She and her husband are still playfully in love, she's running the local PTA like a drill sergeant, they love their new pastor at church, they're involved in two different community organizations, and both kids love school while enjoying a birthday party or scouting event nearly every week-end. But when Sarah looks back on her life, she's filled with a sense of emptiness and regret. Wasn't she supposed to do something great? She imagines her former teachers muttering under their breath, "She's *only* a housewife? What happened?" Sarah attended her twenty-five-year college reunion but avoided her favorite professor, fearful of disappointing him with an "I'm just a mom" life update (she didn't go to graduate school as he had recommended). Sarah has even grown resentful of her husband, whose career has met with success and whose volunteer work at church and in the community is respected by all.

But Sarah "was meant for more," and in her honest, quiet moments she worries that she has missed out on the one great thing for which

God had prepared her. She's convinced herself that she's missed her one true calling, and she grows more resentful and depressed, even while she fulfills the many vocations in which God has placed her with strength and grace.

Both Scott and Sarah illustrate the consequences of believing the myth of vocation (*singular*)—the idea that God purposes each individual for a singular, dramatic job or accomplishment. Scott's case ended in *neglect*. His family, congregation, and community needed his presence and energy—indeed, needed him to see the value of participating in the many vocations (*plural*) God had placed him in. Their lives suffered because of his distraction with the one great thing. Sarah's situation ended in *regret*—she grew disappointed and even resentful because, in her mind, the many activities in which she participated paled in comparison to her destined greatness. Her life seemed a waste—unimportant and unaccomplished—with the haunting questions of "What if?" and "What next?" ever present. In both examples, the ultimate consequence is a disruption of a relationship with God: "Why didn't I listen harder to His voice? Why doesn't He reveal my life's purpose to me? Why can't I hear His voice with more clarity? Why didn't God use me in more dramatic ways?"

Callings

The liberating truth, however, is that we do not have one great calling in life but instead are given many callings simultaneously. Although these may seem small and insignificant, they have sacred worth, given to us by God's own hand. This truth is transformative in that it enables us to participate with joy in life's many relationships, tasks, occupations, and responsibilities knowing that each is a fulfillment of God's purposes. It is His will (or we might say *wills*) for us. To love and serve our neighbor by God's grace and with Christ's forgiveness *is* to do His will and accomplish His purposes. To be sure, there are many inspiring and dramatic examples of God accomplishing great things through people. One thinks of the lives of the saints, or of Christian leaders in our world today whose impact on the Kingdom or society is far-reaching and long-lasting. Certainly, these are gifts to be extolled, sought after, and celebrated in thanksgiving to God. But the reality is, few of us receive such dramatic, earth-changing opportunities; and even the most impactful saints had many and various callings through which God worked His good and gracious will.

Five Heads and Ten Hands

Martin Luther's recovery of the Gospel likewise led to a recovery of a biblical understanding of vocation. Luther redefined *vocatio*, applying it to the variety of God-given tasks, responsibilities, and relationships of the Christian life. Rather than confining it to the one great calling of church work (priests, monks, and nuns), he saw God's Word bringing spiritual significance to the many earthly stations in which the faithful were found. There is not just one great but many greats: *our calling in life is better understood in the plural rather than the singular.*

Writing against the idea that those in the "spiritual estate" (those ordained or those who have taken on holy orders in the Church) were of a higher and holier class, Luther encouraged all Christians to open their eyes to the many ways God already works through them. It's not necessary to encumber oneself with a great, arduous, super-spiritual task in order to be truly doing God's will, Luther argued. In fact, if you begin to take seriously the many ways God already calls you to exercise diligence, love, and service, you might not have time or energy to do anything else.

> How is it possible that you are not called? You have always been in some state or station; you have always been a husband or wife, or boy or girl, or servant. Picture before you the humblest estate. Are you a husband, and you think you have not enough to do in that sphere to govern your wife, children, domestics, and property so that all may be obedient to God and you do no one any wrong? Yea, if you had five heads and ten hands, even then you would be too weak for your

task, so that you would never dare to think of making a pilgrimage or doing any kind of saintly work.[1]

Luther's point is not that we shouldn't do important things for God;
rather, he reminds us that we already are doing them: a five-headed,
ten-handed creature couldn't keep busy enough doing God's work!

Some of the examples Martin Luther uses might seem archaic
to us—most of us don't have servants or operate farms anymore.
All of us, however, have had times when, while seeking after God's
will and purpose, we've been blind to His action and activity already
present. Mowing your elderly neighbor's grass, getting up early to
make a special breakfast for your son on his birthday, helping your
little sister with her math homework, leading an extra study session
before an important exam, encouraging a struggling teammate after
practice—none of this seems particularly dramatic or even spiritual.
All of it, however, is God at work. These activities are no less sacred or
valuable than any one single thing we *feel* God calling us to do—no
matter how dramatic or important it might be.

Indeed, most of the activities and responsibilities of the "five-
headed, ten-handed" Christian wouldn't be listed on a resume. Many
of them might be mentioned in a eulogy, however. In his book *The
Road to Character*, columnist David Brooks from the *New York Times*
makes a distinction between resume virtues and eulogy virtues.[2] When
we're young and ambitious, we like to strive after accomplishments
that advance our status, wealth, power, or influence—anything
that might help us land the next big job, impress our friends, and
intimidate our enemies. Indeed, many of these resume virtues can
be good and God-pleasing. But when we've breathed our last breath
and our bodies are laid to rest, for what things will our loved ones
give thanks with the most affection? Undoubtedly, it will be those
multiple moments through which Christ Himself was active in love

---

1   *The Precious and Sacred Writings of Martin Luther*, ed. John Lenker, vol. 10 (Minneapolis:
Lutherans in All Lands Co., 1905), 242. Reprinted in *The Sermons of Martin Luther*, vol. 1 (Grand
Rapids: Baker, 1989), 242.

2   David Brooks, *The Road to Character* (New York: Random House, 2015), xi.

through us: our eulogy virtues, our callings done in His name, for His glory, and in response to His love. None of these can save us—that's already been done through the blood of Jesus, which forgives us and makes us right before God. But all of them have sacred import and impact, giving us meaning and purpose regardless of how little they're recognized by the world.

Meghan McCain delivered a moving eulogy for her father, Senator John McCain, at his funeral in September 2018. It is hard to imagine a more respected public figure or a more impressive resume: son and grandson of two great admirals; brave POW; decorated war hero; congressman, senator, and presidential candidate. There's even a destroyer in the US Navy that bears the McCain family name. At his funeral, Meghan McCain spoke admirably of these great resume virtues. None of this, however, was of lasting importance to her: "I admired him for all of these great things, but I loved him because he was a great father." Through tears, she listed the many important tasks and dramatic places of his illustrious career, then remarked, "But the best of him was somewhere else. The best of John McCain, the greatest of his titles, and the most important of his roles was as a father." She went on to describe some of the tender moments they shared that would never make any resume: "I know who he was. I know what defined him. I got to see it every single day of my blessed life." In her mind, John McCain was not defined by any of the accomplishments listed on a great resume. "John McCain was defined by love."[3]

Not even the greatest among us (those whose families have ships named after them) and not even the greatest of resumes (those that qualify us for the highest of jobs) can outweigh the sacred worth of exercising love and service in the various callings of our regular life. Every father hopes his children will admire him. But after he is gone, his children will truly cherish the many simple, sacred moments shared in love. In Christ Jesus, we are freed to exercise vocations,

3   "WATCH: Meghan McCain's Complete Eulogy for Her Father, John McCain," PBS News-Hour, accessed November 2, 2019, https://youtu.be/gymd1CScQ88.

callings, through many God-given relationships. Most of these will never be listed on a resume; all of them are fulfilling God's purposes.

Faces, Places, and Spaces

Where, then, do we find our callings (plural), and how can we discover them? There are a dozen courses you can take or hundreds of books you can read; you could hire a spiritual advisor or take a year off to hike in the Himalayas. There is a simpler and better way to start, however. Look to the *faces*, *places*, and *spaces* of your life. Whom do you encounter on a daily basis? Where do you live, study, work, worship, and play? What roles do you have at home, school, work, church, and society? Because you believe in Jesus and have been baptized into His life, death, and resurrection, you are loved and freed for all eternity. What is more, God is already, even now, working through you in the lives of others. Your callings are plural, not singular, and they already have begun.

THE PEOPLE THAT YOU MEET
WHEN YOU'RE WALKING DOWN THE STREET

Jamal's phone woke him early for practice. His roommate was still sleeping, so he carefully and quietly put on his workout clothes in the dark and laced up his Nikes. It had been a rough weekend for his roommate—a couple of poor choices were made and a messy relationship finally came to a hard and hurtful end. Jamal took a moment to text him an encouraging Bible passage, knowing it would be the first thing seen before his 8:00 a.m. class: "Fear not, for I have redeemed you; I have called you by name, you are Mine" (Isaiah 43:1). Before he left the room, Jamal spent an extra few minutes in prayer for his friend, whom he knew had a tough day ahead.

After quietly leaving the room, Jamal ran into his RA (resident assistant) in the hallway. They were both in a hurry but paused long enough for Jamal to thank him for last week's floor program. Not a lot of guys showed up, so Jamal thought he could use a bit of encouragement. Jogging out of the residence hall, Jamal saw one of the college maintenance workers on early morning trash duty. Jamal greeted him by name and asked about his daughter's first day of preschool. The worker gave a smile and a thumbs-up, and Jamal fired the same back as he sprinted off to practice.

As captain of the basketball team, Jamal knew how important it was to set an example of leadership. He set up the cones for a defensive drill before the coach arrived and took a moment to chat with two of the new freshmen on the team. They were both far from home and having some trouble adjusting. Jamal invited them over for some PlayStation after lunch and reminded them that the team was going to chapel later that morning for worship.

After practice, Jamal took a few minutes to chat with the coach. Some of the guys were frustrated about the new offense, and he wanted to address it directly, right away, before any problems surfaced. A quick shower, an OJ and bagel from the cafeteria, and he sat down just in time for his 8:00 a.m. class. The professor was new, so she struggled *again* with the technology for the lecture. Jamal popped up from his desk and adjusted something quickly on her laptop so the PowerPoint would work. He gave his teammates snickering in the back row a stern look to quiet them down, and the lecture proceeded flawlessly.

By only 8:05 a.m., Jamal already demonstrated love, service, and sacrifice in a number of his God-given callings. Each individual face seen that morning was a sacred vocation, an opportunity for Christ to be at work through him. He had been a friend giving the Word, a classmate offering encouragement, a captain displaying responsibility, and a student showing respect. Jamal needed little help in discovering his God-given purpose. He simply looked into the faces of his normal morning routine.

Each of us has a number of relationships that can be regarded as God-callings. In order to discern them, we need simply ask, "Who is in my life? Whom do I encounter on a daily basis?" The people that you meet when you're walking down the street are as good a place as any to begin. The first faces of each new day are a calling—your family members or those with whom you live. God has given them to you. Although we often overlook these essential callings because they seem ordinary and commonplace, they are usually the most important vocations we have.

We then might encounter our co-workers or classmates. Although they're seldom as close to us as our own families, they nonetheless have been placed in our life by God and are a sacred calling—even the people we don't like or who rub us the wrong way. Some we encounter more casually or occasionally—the next-door neighbor who generally keeps to herself or the retired man in the apartment across the hall.

Lastly, there are the random faces we encounter that we may never see again—the person in line behind us at the grocery store who looks like he's had a rough day; the woman who just cut us off in traffic (ouch!); a family having car trouble along the highway on a rainy night. Jesus Himself labels these as your neighbor in the parable of the Good Samaritan (Luke 10:25–37).

Not all the faces we encounter are the same type of calling, nor should they demand from us equal time, energy, and attention. Yet these people are individually sacred because the Father created them out of love and redeemed them in the work of His Son on the cross. Our job is to see them as Christ does. We may never run into them again or know the harvest of a seed planted in a seemingly random encounter; nevertheless, we are to regard each of them as a divine calling, an opportunity to express vocation. You never know what one small act of love, done in Jesus' name, might mean. All our callings begin with faces—people in relationship to us, equally broken and sinful, but equally redeemed and loved by God.

. . . .

I have community with others and will continue to have it only through Jesus Christ. The more genuine and the deeper our community becomes, the more everything else between us will recede, and the more clearly and purely will Jesus Christ and his work become the one and only thing that is alive between us. We have one another only through Christ, but through Christ we really do *have* one another. We have one another completely and for all eternity.[4] DIETRICH BONHOEFFER

. . . .

PLACES

Every *face* we encounter is an opportunity to exercise vocation, but so is every *place* where we live, study, work, worship, or play. Thinking in the broadest terms, we're all obviously residents of planet Earth—citizens of the world, so to speak. We are thus fellow creatures with the whole created order and certainly fellow children of our Creator-Father, the almighty God, who made us each in His image and gifted us with infinite worth. We have a shared humanity through the First Article of the Creed—"God has made me and all creatures," as Luther explained in his Small Catechism. This implies a vocation as a human being in the care and concern for every other human being. Issues of poverty, injustice, and the neglect of the disadvantaged and marginalized, both at home and abroad, should be our great concern not simply because our Christian duty is to love but also because we share a common humanity with all. In the broadest sense, we remain a neighbor to all.

4   Dietrich Bonhoeffer, *Dietrich Bonhoeffer Works*, vol. 5, *Life Together* and *Prayer Book of the Bible*, ed. Geffrey B. Kelly (Minneapolis: Fortress Press, 2005), 34.

Because of our presence on planet Earth, we also have a calling to the nonhuman creation. The earth is ours to care for and tend, as did Adam and Eve in the garden. Christians are rightly concerned about some of the more extreme ideologies of the modern environmental movement. Consequently, some have exercised caution in getting involved with local or national initiatives. It is worth noting, however, that historic Christianity has always recognized that care for God's creation, in its both micro and macro aspects, is not only permitted but commanded by God. Recognizing planet Earth as one of the *places* you occupy is an avenue for right responsibility, for exercising a calling toward all of God's good creation—human and nonhuman.

As Christians who embrace the gift of our creatureliness we need to learn to live as creatures. . . . This means we accept that we are part of a whole interconnected web of life within which each creature is a gift to the other. We see our lives as human creatures defined not by the freedom to exceed limits in the pursuit of personal fulfillment but by the freedom to limit ourselves for the sake of the other.[5]

Another *place* we occupy is a nation. As individual citizens who reside in a particular country, we have a responsibility to be engaged in civic and political life. But in what ways should a Christian be involved in government? The simplistic answer is the quip "Pray, Pay, and Obey"—pray for the government, pay your taxes, and obey the laws as from God. This is, indeed, quite true—we *are* called to do these things. But as residents of a nation, our calling must also mean more than this.

5   The Commission on Theology and Church Relations, *Together with All Creatures: Caring for God's Living Earth* (St. Louis: The Lutheran Church—Missouri Synod, 2010), 84.

Another threefold way of talking about Christian engagement in the laws of the land might be "Make, Take, and Break." The laws we *make*, we make out of reverence to God and love for our neighbor. Thus, Christians have a calling to engage fully in the democratic process, promoting the God-given values of equity, justice, peace, and good order in the legislative process, while also supporting political candidates who promote and protect these values. The laws we *take* (that is, those we accept or obey), we take out of respect toward God and love for our neighbor. St. Paul's chapter on earthly authority (Romans 13:1–7) does not permit us to follow only those laws we like, those personally preferable to us, but rather commands us to willingly submit to those in authority so long as they do not contradict the Word of God. Finally, the laws we *break*, we break out of respect toward God and love toward our neighbor. Civil disobedience is also part of our Christian heritage and is certainly biblical. Daniel, one of the highest leaders of King Darius's government, refused to follow or enforce an idolatrous law (Daniel 6). Peter and the disciples received imprisonment and beatings because they chose to obey God rather than men by preaching Christ (Acts 5). *Breaking* laws may at times be the necessary and noble calling of a Christian, who likewise must be willing to suffer the consequences of any godly disobedience. Simply because of *where* we live—we are residents of a particular country— we are called to be engaged fully in the democratic process in our making, taking, and possibly even breaking of our nation's laws, if they oppose the clear teaching of Scripture.

A PRAYER FOR THOSE IN AUTHORITY

Eternal Lord, ruler of all, graciously regard those who have been set in positions of authority among us that, guided by Your Spirit, they may be high in purpose, wise in counsel, firm in good resolution, and unwavering in duty, that under them we may be governed quietly and peaceably; through Jesus Christ, our Lord. Amen.[6]

You live in a nation but also a community. Participating in local government, volunteering at the community library, attending community events such as the Fourth of July parade or the summer music festival all are ways through which God's providential hand extends into the structures of society. You're likewise a neighbor in your neighborhood, whether your home is a two-story Georgian on an oak-lined parkway, the upper level of a two-flat residence, a downtown high-rise, a studio apartment in an assisted-living facility, or a shared room in a residence hall. Christians fulfill important callings in every place they reside, being salt and light (Matthew 5:13–16) through witness, service, and friendship. A Christian family helps an elderly couple by taking out their trash every Monday morning. A young professional makes it a point of going to the condo association's block party. A young mom welcomes the other neighborhood kids into her home for regular playdates. A high school student makes room at the lunch table for the new kid. These can seem insignificant and even inconvenient or bothersome, but wherever God places you, He also calls you. These are often the most life-impacting callings we have.

....

6   *Pastoral Care Companion* (St. Louis: Concordia Publishing House, 2007), 637.

For most of the history of Christianity, people did not choose their church. Born in a particular region, citizens were more or less stuck with a default worshiping community. It would have been inconvenient and awkward to simply choose a different place of worship to better fit your needs. In Martin Luther's day, for example, a congregation was not something for which you shopped around and eventually decided to join. It was assigned to you by *where* you lived and usually remained a part of your family history for generations.

Modern Western Christians enjoy the freedom to choose where we work, what we buy, and the people with whom we associate. There are unquestionably many social and economic benefits to this—aren't you glad you don't *have* to do the same work as your parents or live in the same house for the rest of your life? But one of the consequences of our freedom to worship is that church members tend to see their congregation as a product for their personal consumption rather than a *place* they're called to be. If you begin to see your home church as a calling rather than a choice—a vocation given by God—then you'll also begin seeking the Spirit's fruit of love, joy, peace, patience, and gentleness in order to fulfill this calling. A congregation is a place where you worship, receive God's Word of life, and grow in knowledge and godliness. It is also a place of calling.

> *But the fruit of the Spirit is love, joy, peace, patience, kindness, goodness, faithfulness, gentleness, self-control; against such things there is no law.* (GALATIANS 5:22–23)

Your foundational calling, without a doubt, remains as a baptized child of God—a calling you have received through *the* Church Universal. But at the particular congregation where you dwell on Sundays (and hopefully other days of the week), you serve as an extension of God's love to others. And since it's a place of calling—the Lord has put you there for a reason and for a season—He certainly will bless you with the gifts of energy, endurance, charity, and fellowship necessary for such a calling.

The most essential place of calling we have, however, is our home. In Martin Luther's time, the home remained a place of both rest and work. Since the vast majority of economic activity came from agriculture, the job was the farm, which also was the family, which also was the residence. It's no wonder then that Luther spoke so frequently about the callings of work and rest, family and spouse, workers and animals.

- -

He also gives me clothing and shoes, food and drink, house and home, wife and children, land, animals, and all I have. He richly and daily provides me with all that I need to support this body and life. SMALL CATECHISM, FIRST ARTICLE

- -

Our homes are different today. Most of us leave and go off to work or school and then return at the end of the day. Although more people are working where they live—a small business run out of a house or an employee working remotely via the internet—it remains true that we think of work and home as distinctive spheres of activity.

Too often, we neglect this essential place, this grounded calling of home. We might even see it as a distraction or diversion from the "real work" that needs to be done. Our home lives can seem so ordinary, monotonous, and unexciting compared to the great callings and accomplishments "out there" in the Church or society. Nothing could be further from the truth. Other than our baptismal calling, no other vocation shapes us, and in turn is used by God to shape others, as intimately and powerfully as our home-calling.

A single mom works tirelessly to keep it all together and maintain a sense of normalcy after her husband abruptly leaves them. A successful father turns down a prestigious job because it would mean less time with his kids. Stepbrothers make an extra effort to get along and help around the house. A big sister rises early and makes the lunches because Mom is in the hospital again. A preschooler gives Dad an extra hug, knowing he's had a difficult day. Each of these examples requires a measure of sacrifice and is often done instinctively. Although they'll never make the headlines, without a doubt God works through these servants in the essential place where their earthly callings begin—the home.

- -

A PRAYER FOR OUR HOMES

O God, our dwelling place in all generations, look with favor upon the homes of our land. Embrace husbands and wives, parents and children, in the arms of Your love, and grant that each, in reverence for Christ, fulfill the duties You have given. Bless our homes that they may ever be a shelter for the defenseless, a fortress for the tempted, a resting place for the weary, and a foretaste of our eternal home with You; through Jesus Christ, Your Son, our Lord, who lives and reigns with You and the Holy Spirit, one God, now and forever. Amen.[7]

- -

SPACES

The *faces* we encounter, the *places* we live, and the *spaces* we occupy teem with opportunities to fulfill God's purposes—to be the hands and heart of Jesus for others. These three spheres certainly overlap— think of three overlapping circles or three different windows viewing the same room. You encounter the *who* in the *where*—a classmate is seen at your school, for example. By *spaces*, however, we mean the

----

7   *Lutheran Service Book: Agenda* (St. Louis: Concordia Publishing House, 2006), 70.

what. What are the roles you play in society, the positions you hold, the offices you occupy, or the responsibilities you've been given? Each of these also carries with it a calling from God.

Some *spaces*, or roles we fulfill in society, are ours by default. You're a big brother because your parents had more children after you were born—you didn't have much choice in the matter. Your voice rises above others at the congregational voters meeting because your grandparents were founding members. You're asked to lead a capital campaign because, having inherited a great deal of wealth, your family has been generous for generations. The family store has sat on that corner for half a century, so the community seeks your opinion on important matters. Each of these examples comes with both rights and responsibilities, blessings and burdens. To see them as ultimately given by God removes them from the realm of roles we possess for ourselves and into an opportunity for stewardship and service.

Other positions we hold are opportunities that are given to us. The school principal asks a capable mom to head up the Parent-Teacher Association because she has drive and energy. The varsity coach approaches a young man with natural leadership skills to serve as captain of the team next year. The dean of the college taps a seasoned professor to spearhead a new academic initiative. The vice president of the company appoints a capable employee to chair an important committee. Each of these *spaces*, these roles in an organization, comes with additional prestige and respect. Some might even include an increase in pay. But by regarding them as one of many calling*s* given by God, they become opportunities for servant-leadership rather than self-promotion.

A number of the roles we play in society come from our own initiative. Although these are self-chosen, they nonetheless should be regarded as an opportunity to exercise vocation. A student *chooses* to join an athletic team. This brings with it a lot of fun, a close-knit group of friends, and the joys of camaraderie and competition that physical exercise brings. But it also means hard work, perseverance, sacrifice for the team, and an unselfish attitude in games and practice.

To be a member of a team, regardless of your skill level or playing time, is to occupy a *space* in your school or community.

A young person decides to join the military. This has a number of advantages, such as steady income, respect in society, money for college, and the opportunity for adventure and travel. But when seen as a calling, it is unquestionably a sacred burden resulting in tremendous strain on the family and much self-sacrifice. Serving in the military is a legitimate calling from God because it is a *space* one occupies in society, a publicly recognized role. There are ways to fail at this calling—laziness, disobedience, using your rank or position for self-serving ends, or disrespecting the uniform and the nation you represent through unruly public or private behavior. There are also a multitude of ways military service can be a sincere response of faith: exhibiting the virtues of integrity, bravery, self-sacrifice, honor, and upright living. All who serve in the Armed Forces agree that these are virtues for which to strive; the Christian seeks them as response to God's love and in recognition of His good and gracious activity.

A PRAYER FOR THOSE SERVING IN A NATION'S ARMED FORCES

Lord God Almighty, we give You thanks for our loved ones' service and dedication to their country. We pray for Your presence with them in travel and training, at work and at rest, granting to them Your protection and a renewed sense of the calling to serve. We ask that You would grant success to their missions, according to Your will. We pray for Your peace to rest upon them in times of war and rumors of war, and for You to bring a true and lasting peace to all the children of the earth, through Jesus Christ, our Lord. Amen.

Response-ability

Blanca loved her new school. The small Christian college where she could be involved in a number of activities was the perfect fit for her. As the first person in her family ever to attend college, she felt an incredible amount of pressure to succeed. Almost daily, she thought about the sacrifices her parents were making to give her this opportunity. Double shifts at work, picking her up late at night after class, and cosigning on her student loan all expressed their incredible love and confidence in her. She worked hard at her studies and grew academically and spiritually in her first couple of years. Blanca understood how much God had done for her, not only through the Gospel of salvation and forgiveness in Jesus, but also through her parents' dedication and sacrifice. She began to feel the responsibility of using all that she'd been given to make a difference for others. When the president's position with the school's Latino Student Union became vacant, Blanca stepped up. Although it would mean significant challenges—more meetings, fundraising, garnering enthusiasm, recruiting volunteers, and working with the college's administration—she saw it as a perfect opportunity to use her gifts in service to others in response to all God had done for her. This was a calling and a vocation from God—one of many she already had and one she chose for herself.

One of the most important self-chosen roles we play in society is that of our occupation, or employment. As we have seen, this is but one of many of our vocations, yet because of the amount of time spent at our job, how much we rely on it for our livelihood, and how much of ourselves we invest in it, our paid work is of great personal significance. Christians, however, have a spiritual view of their work and positions. They regard their talents and abilities as gifts from God rather than solely personal achievements. Their income is entrusted to them for good stewardship rather than for personal gain and selfish use. When given authority over others, it is exercised not from a perspective of pride or the need to control but for the good of others and the benefit of the organization. Menial tasks are done cheerfully, prestigious ones humbly, and every activity with the knowledge that we are accountable ultimately to God.

Gifted Callings

The *faces*, *places*, and *spaces* of our lives are not random and purposeless, nor are they indulgent opportunities for personal advancement or gain. God introduces various people into your daily walk and places you in a plethora of earthly relationships. God grounds you in a home, a community, a school, a church, a nation, and a created world. God gives you roles and responsibilities; positions and promotions; tasks and talents; stations and seasons in life. When seen as *gifts*, they begin to take on sacred, joyful importance. How amazing to think that the almighty God is even now at work through you, in the multitude of callings you have right now! You don't need to search tirelessly and needlessly after the one great thing. You already have many great things unfolding in the *who*, the *where*, and the *what* of daily life.

Sometimes these things change (most of the time they do). Callings are not static. And each of them comes with both blessings and burdens—things we love and celebrate about them and things that make them challenging and difficult. But when we truly reflect on our lives, we can see how many different callings God has indeed given us. It is easy to see how focusing on the one great thing is not so great. It causes us to miss opportunities to show God's love right in front of us—who we meet, where we live, and what we do. In each of these spheres, God is at work through us in important but sometimes hidden ways. The Christian recognizes this, celebrates it, and seeks God's Spirit for the strength and grace to fulfill these many vocations according to His will and for His glory.

Baptismal Callings

How exciting to discover the many ways God is at work through me! I have callings. I don't have to exhaust my energy seeking after the one great thing. God has given me meaningful and holy relationships, roles, and activities presently that are pleasing to Him and fulfilling for me—if only I would open my eyes and embrace them. Knowing this relieves the tremendous pressure of trying to discern that single, seismic, sacred, self-fulfilling thing that God has placed me on this earth to accomplish: "How do I know what it is? Where can I find it? What if I miss it? Will I ever fully live up to the task?" But when I begin to understand that my callings are found in the plural rather than the singular, I can live at ease and at peace, expressing love and service in the *faces, places,* and *spaces* of my God-given life.

Seeing vocation in the plural rather than the singular is also fulfilling in light of the many and diverse ways God works through me. I am not just called to be an employee, nor is my worth solely determined by income or societal status. Being a good neighbor, when done in faith, is just as valued by God. Striving to be the best big brother in the world is no less important than being president. A husband and father cannot be valued simply by how much money he brings to the family. Working to fulfill the varied callings we have opens up a rich diversity of ways to express the Christian life. There's nothing boring about the plural! In the diversity of people I encounter or the varied places God sends me or the multiple roles I am given, God's life and love work through me.

Seeing vocation this way, however, also brings significant challenges. How do I balance and prioritize my many callings? A high school student wants to have a dating relationship, maintain good friendships, run cross-country, tour with the choir, serve on student council, get good grades, and occasionally check in at home with Mom and Dad for nourishment. When we acknowledge all of these activities and relationships as God-given and thus possessing sacred responsibility, we also can easily feel overwhelmed. How do I fulfill *all* this? If they were unimportant or unrelated to my faith, then any one of them could be easily set aside, put on pause, or disregarded as insignificant or optional. But because I recognize God at work through me in these various ways, it can be exhausting stewarding my time, energy, and attention.

Trying to balance many callings is certainly a challenge, but so is the constant failure at all of them. As we begin to perceive the multiple ways God expects us to be His instruments, we also note the multifaceted ways we've fallen far short of these expectations: I haven't taken good care of the planet; I haven't applied myself at work or in my studies; I've neglected my family and neighbors; I've dropped the ball with my responsibilities; I've conducted myself with bitterness and resentment rather than cheerfulness and thankfulness. Understanding vocation in the plural rather than the singular convicts and overwhelms us because it rightly exposes the fact that we've departed from God in many ways, not just one. What is more, our neighbor in need—the very one God placed in our life for us to serve—suffers because of our sinful neglect.

As convicting as this might be, we find good news when we return to our one, most essential calling as baptized children of God. This is the "one" from which the "many" flow. In Baptism, the Holy Spirit grafts us into the life, death, and resurrection of Jesus Christ, our Savior. This means all He has done and accomplished flows to us fully, freely, and through faith. By taking on our flesh and blood, Christ Jesus perfectly completed all that needs to be accomplished. *All* of it. Every person who needs to be loved, every task that needs to be completed, every attitude that needs to be changed, Christ as the perfect human already has done *for us*. No fuller, more obedient, more complete life could ever be lived than the life of Jesus. The fullness of this life flows over us and into us freely, as a covering for all our sin, when we believe and are baptized. In the incarnation, the Son of God has not only opened up the value of our many callings (the *faces*, *places*, and *spaces*) and declared them good, holy, valuable, and God-pleasing, he has also redeemed our many failings in those callings.

Grant us, O God, the strength and courage
  To live the faith our lips declare;
Bless us in our baptismal calling;
  Christ's royal priesthood help us share.
Turn us from ev'ry false allegiance,
  That we may trust in Christ alone:
Raise up in us a chosen people
  Transformed by love to be Your own.[8]

LSB 600:3

In His death on the cross, Jesus Christ's shed blood gives us ongoing forgiveness for the many ways we fail at our vocations. As many as our failings, so much greater is His forgiveness. By His wounds on the cross, by His bitter sufferings and death, Jesus Christ bore the full punishment of God for us. For those who believe and are baptized into His name, not one drop of wrath or responsibility remains. "It is finished" (John 19:30). Because nothing else needs to be earned, accomplished, or achieved, Christians can in freedom and faith, with peace and power, seek to love and serve their neighbor in the various relationships and response-abilities of a redeemed life.[9] As it is sometimes put, "Now that you don't *have* to do anything, what are you going to do?"

Jesus Christ did not stay dead but arose victoriously to bring new life to all. By rising on the third day, the Lord declared victory over the last and greatest enemy, death. He lives now and reigns over all creation, promising to return one day to gather together all who trust in Him into the bliss of eternal life. By His victorious life, Jesus Christ

8   Hymn text: Carl P. Daw Jr. © 1990 Hope Publishing Company, Carol Stream, IL 60188. All rights reserved. Used by permission.

9   I owe the insightful misspelling of "response-ability" to Robert Kolb, "Called to Milk Cows and Govern Kingdoms: Martin Luther's Teaching on the Christian's Vocations," *Concordia Journal* (Spring 2013): 134.

has also won us full forgiveness for all our sins—for the many ways we fail Him in our earthly vocations. He has pronounced us perfect, declared us righteous before God because of all He accomplished for our salvation.

> We know that Christ is raised and dies no more.
> Embraced by death, He broke its fearful hold;
> And our despair He turned to blazing joy.
> Alleluia!
>
> We share by water in His saving death.
> Reborn, we share with Him an Easter life
> As living members of a living Christ.
> Alleluia!
>
> The Father's splendor clothes the Son with life.
> The Spirit's power shakes the Church of God.
> Baptized, we live with God the Three in One.
> Alleluia! [10]
>
> *LSB 603*

All of this is true, for God has told us this in His Word, the Holy Scriptures. Thus, the work of my many callings accomplishes nothing for my standing before God; they are not required to be fulfilled in order for me to achieve salvation and peace. I don't need to be doing anything "for God." Rather, the life Christ lived I now can live without guilt or obligation in the life of my neighbor in need. I am freed to get lost in the living out of the life of Christ in the multiple callings God gives. Because we remain in the fallen world and are not yet free from our sinful selves, we continually need to return to the forgiveness of our baptismal callings, renewed by God's Word and Sacraments. God the Holy Spirit works through these gifts to bring us the assurance of

---

10   Hymn text: © John B. Geyer. All rights reserved. Used by permission.

forgiveness but also to strengthen us in joy to serve others through the many callings He gives us.

> O Christian, firmly hold this gift
>   And give God thanks forever!
> It gives the power to uplift
>   In all that you endeavor.
> When nothing else revives your soul,
> Your Baptism stands and makes you whole
>   And then in death completes you.
>
> So use it well! You are made new—
>   In Christ a new creation!
> As faithful Christians, live and do
>   Within your own vocation,
> Until that day when you possess
> His glorious robe of righteousness
>   Bestowed on you forever!
>
> *LSB* 596:5–6

For Discussion

1. What is the myth of the "one great thing" (pages 1–2, 6)?

2. How might the distinction between resume and eulogy virtues (page 8) change the way you prioritize your life?

3. Why do you think Martin Luther's redefinition of *vocatio* was so impactful?

4. List the number of callings Jamal encounters in the "faces" of his morning (pages 10–11). Take a random day in your life and do the same.

5. What are ways a Christian can, in good conscience, exercise his or her calling as a citizen of planet Earth?

6. What new law might you want to pass to better serve society? Can you think of laws you disagree with that you nevertheless obey out of respect for authority? Can you imagine a time or circumstance that would force you to disobey the government?

7. What are the most challenging callings you're currently struggling with?

8. If you couldn't simply choose or unchoose your particular congregation or place of worship, how might that change the way you would view its work and ministry?

9. How does Blanca's example (page 22) inspire you to take initiative in serving others?

10. What's different about a Christian's view of his or her job or occupation (pages 22–23)?

11. Discuss the challenges inherent in balancing many different callings.

12. Why is your baptismal calling described as your "most essential calling" (page 25)?

JANUS.

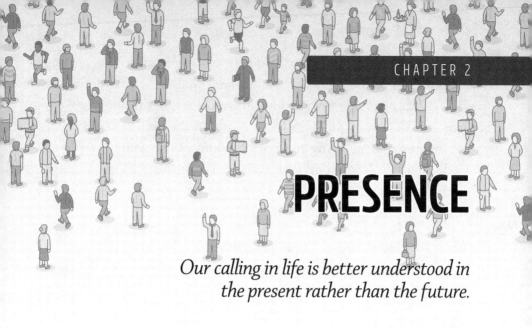

CHAPTER 2

PRESENCE

Our calling in life is better understood in the present rather than the future.

Worshiping Janus

Janus, the Roman god of doorways, faced backward and forward at the same time. His two faces on one torso enabled him to see both behind and before, making his image a popular choice in the archways, entrances, and exits of the ancient world. The main temple erected to him in Rome stretched from east to west, marking both the beginning and the ending of the day. The two doors on either end of the temple were closed only during times of peace—a rare occurrence indeed over the centuries of Roman conquest. Janus could rest only when Rome was at rest.

The name of our first month, January, comes from this exceptionally popular god. His ability to fixate simultaneously upon the past and the future, what has already happened and what will soon take place, and the enemies both behind and before, made his double face a constant presence across the empire. Janus is easily spotted on any tourist trip to Rome or during a visit to the Classical World wing of any major museum.

Although few worship literal statues anymore, the lure of the false god Janus remains just as enticing today. How difficult it is to just be present, to embrace the callings of our current life without constantly looking backward and forward at the same time. In his explanation of the First Commandment, Martin Luther defined a false god as anything we fear, love, and trust above the one true God. This insight locates the sin of idolatry not in the item worshiped but in the human heart. Anything can become a false god if it replaces God's rightful place in our lives, even (and especially) the good things God has given us.

* *

You shall have no other gods. *What does this mean?* We should fear, love, and trust in God above all things. SMALL CATECHISM, FIRST COMMANDMENT

* *

The worship of Janus is alive and well today in the constant fixation upon either the past or future and in our refusal to simply be at peace in the present, knowing the God who knows all and promises to be with us in all things.

Facing Backward—Worshiping the Past

Aaron couldn't free himself from it. He would wake up in the middle of the night with a sea of shame encompassing him. Although he had confessed, heard the assurance of forgiveness, received the Lord's Supper, and read the words of Christ's forgiveness numerous times, the crippling guilt of his past transgressions remained. During high school and college, Aaron did not live the life of a Christian. He turned his back on the solid upbringing of his church and family, wasting years in drunkenness, partying, and sexual adventures. The worst feelings of guilt stemmed not from the damage he did to himself— Aaron was still dealing with the physical and emotional consequences of his past sins—but rather from his treatment of others. He came to realize the self-centered and self-indulgent nature of so many of his relationships. In those dark days, people had become merely objects for his own gratification emotionally, socially, and sexually.

Reflecting on this dark period of his life, Aaron could hardly imagine a more un-Christlike life.

Things were different now, thankfully. Months of rehab and counseling, moving back home to live with disappointed but forgiving parents, the renewal of his childhood faith, and a reengagement in his home parish all came together to bring health and healing. The past was the past. A new chapter began. Forgive and forget, right? That's the way it's supposed to work, but Aaron wasn't so sure. When his pastor pulled him aside after worship one Sunday and asked him to prayerfully consider going into ministry, Aaron recoiled almost in anger. Didn't Pastor know Aaron's past—how far he had fallen and how selfish he had been? Surely his own pastor could see how unqualified he was for any kind of ministry or work in the church! His pastor's overtures seemed to Aaron either an insensitive joke or blatant mockery.

His pastor's attempt to plant a seed in Aaron's heart about ministry only renewed a sense of guilt. Specific moments and memories of a sinful past reappeared at the most inopportune times. Aaron would shudder, shake his head, and curse at himself under his breath when reminded of all he'd done. It almost felt to him like someone . . . or *something* . . . had a hold of his head, forcing him to stare at the multitude of failings that disqualified him for ministry.

Aaron was worshiping Janus, the god of doorways. Although he was forgiven and set free by the work of Christ Jesus and covered in His righteousness as a gift, Aaron's obsession with a guilt-filled past led to trusting in it rather than the God of grace and forgiveness. Aaron's was a form of the sin of idolatry that exists in so many of us. Guilt can be good, of course. God's Law in the Scriptures is indeed meant to convict us, bring us to repentance, and lead us into the arms of our Savior. But there is also a satanic use of God's good Law—to keep us away from Christ and in constant despair and inactivity. Janus's backward face wants us to stare at our sins and shortcomings and in shame remain there, even when we have repented and been assured of Christ's forgiveness. One of the most common and destructive forms of worshiping the past is living unnecessarily in guilt and disappointment. At its worst, it is dismissive of the power and love of Christ's work on the cross. My sinful past becomes more important than my Savior's sacrifice for me—a false, backward-facing god indeed.

REPRISTINATION LUTHERAN CHURCH

Trinity Lutheran Church and School had its glory days—and the old guard of church leadership is quick to remind you of it whenever possible. The congregation grew so fast after the building of its original sanctuary that an expanded worship space was soon needed—and was dedicated debt-free, by the way. The excitement, energy, and activities of Sunday School rally days are legendary. The kids *always* loved to be there and *never* misbehaved. The Day School had two classrooms per grade during its heyday; its state basketball championships and outstanding music and dramatic performances never eclipsed the school's academic rigor. Vacation Bible School reached such popularity in the community that *two* summer sessions were needed and over three hundred lunches were prepared daily (the children also ate *all* their vegetables, you'll be glad to know).

Everyone remembers with fondness and respect Pastor Schmidtke, shepherd at Trinity for nearly thirty years. His involvement in the neighborhood, his ever-full new member classes, his moving reading of John 1 on Christmas Eve, and the way the congregation flourished under his leadership remain topics of conversation even after three other pastors have come and gone since his retirement. It is rumored that even the angels wept during one of his moving Good Friday sermons. No mortal will ever measure up to Saint Schmidtke.

Mrs. Schmidtke (*Frau Pastor*—to some of the oldest ladies at Trinity) matched her husband in energy but surpassed him in wit and charm. Always put together, always graceful, always present in friendship and fellowship, it's hard to imagine the pastor's ministry meeting with such success without Mrs. Schmidtke at his side. None of the three subsequent pastors' wives had come even close to her Christian example and leadership. She also led the choir, by the way, which has never been as good since (she didn't get paid for directing, either, in case you were wondering).

The fellowship meals of Trinity's golden era reached biblical proportions *and* biblical portions. The congregation's seventy-fifth anniversary fed more than eight hundred (the number keeps rising). If you listen carefully on a quiet afternoon, you can almost hear the lick-smacking from Grandpa Hale's beef brisket still echoing around the rafters of the church hall. The number, variety, and quality of pies consumed that day have never been fully quantified but, rest assured, will never be matched again this side of the Second Coming. No food was ever wasted, no gossip was ever spoken, and cleaning up afterward was always done cheerfully without conflict or complaint.

Trinity's golden past is not just in the past, unfortunately. A fixation on the past, attempts to reestablish it, and constant comparisons to the church's present ministry have made new initiatives and new energy impossible. The congregation's attempts at *repristination*—seeking to restore a lost, golden, and more "pristine" era—have caused it to fall into a Janus-like idolatry. The Sunday School will never be good enough because of the lack of numbers—no matter how faithful its teaching or teachers. No new building or renovation project can ever be approved if a loan must be secured. No pastor's sermon, however Christ-centered and edifying it might be, can compare to Saint Schmitdke's. No outreach efforts will ever be good enough, no choir will ever sing beautifully enough, no church worker will ever labor hard enough (or cheaply enough), and no meal will ever be bountiful enough to measure up to the glory days of years past.

The problems with Trinity's attempts at repristination are threefold. First, the past was never as good as some remember it, so trying to restore it might not be that great of an idea anyway. Plenty of conflicts arose on the church council; neither the teachers nor the students of the school were ever perfect. Schmidtke had plenty of sermons that were duds. And no one likes to recall that one inglorious potluck that ended in food poisoning for a couple of dozen members. Looking back with affection and nostalgia tends to skew our perceptions of the past.

Second, even if you wanted to restore the past, it's impossible to do so. The world changes, culture changes, and people change such that no particular moment in a congregation's history is reproducible, even if this were desirable. Ultimately, only the Word of the Lord endures forever. The Church's mission is to reach out to this quickly changing world with the unchanging nature of Christ's Gospel. It won't, and indeed *can't*, look the same in each subsequent generation.

> *The grass withers, the flower fades, but the word of our God will stand forever.* (ISAIAH 40:8)

Third, the attempt to return to a certain glorious past itself can be idolatrous. It is Christ Jesus who is Lord of the Church, and He alone is to receive our worship, thanks, and praise. Our glorification of an unattainable past can at times replace Christ Himself. It is, of course, normal and even necessary at times to look backward with wisdom, reflection, and thanksgiving. Staring Janus-like at the past, however, becomes a false god when the past or the attempt to retrieve, reproduce, or replicate it becomes more important than Christ and the work He's given us today.

We see, then, how both *guilt* (in Aaron's case) and *glorification* (in Trinity's case) can arise from an idolatrous obsession with the past. Both responses can be good—repenting of one's past sins; thanking God for a congregation's rich history—but when they eclipse the present calling and work of Christ among us and hinder its flourishing, they become no better than a two-faced Roman god worshiped centuries ago.

©shutterstock.com/Claudio Divizia

Facing Forward—Worshiping the Future

The Roman god of doorways stared into both the past and the future. His ability to know both simultaneously, to protect against enemies behind and before, made him one of the more popular gods of the ancient world. We have seen how destructive our own obsession with the past can be, especially when it counteracts the word and work of Christ Himself.

Equally dangerous, however, is the false god of the future—the forward-staring face of Janus. This false god can take a number of forms, but the most prevalent is that of godless anxiety. By always looking ahead and never resting in the present, we become hindered with constant fear, worry, and uncertainty. A thousand doubts and what-ifs arise as we pay homage to the future: "What if I fail, I sin, or something doesn't go exactly according to plan? What if tragedy strikes, an endeavor isn't successful, or I fall flat on my face trying? What if I'm rejected, made fun of, or even persecuted for the truth?" The more we obsess about the future, the more possible negative outcomes we fear, the more uncertain we become, and the more likely we cannot proceed in faith and love. The fear of failure or the discomfort over the possibility of something not working out derails us into faithless inactivity. Our eyes become fixated on the future rather than the One who holds the future—Christ Jesus Himself.

> *Rejoice in the Lord always; again I will say, rejoice. Let your reasonableness be known to everyone. The Lord is at hand; do not be anxious about anything, but in everything by prayer and supplication with thanksgiving let your requests be made known to God. And the peace of God, which surpasses all understanding, will guard your hearts and your minds in Christ Jesus.*
>
> (PHILIPPIANS 4:4–7)

But there is something worse than the anxiety-inducing worship of the future: the neglect of one's present callings at the expense of a mythic, one great calling we imagine for ourselves in the future. Like chapter 1, which warned against seeing vocation in the singular rather than the plural, here the caution is against fixating on the future at the expense of the present. By obsessing Janus-like in anticipation of a future great job, relationship, event, or accomplishment, we easily neglect the multitude of opportunities for love and service God is currently placing before us. What is more, like our gods of the past, our gods of the future seldom actually meet our expectations of meaning and personal fulfillment. Like all false gods, they consume us, betray us, and ultimately destroy us.

It is, of course, normal and necessary at times to look ahead with preparation or anticipation, and certainly no life is lived anxiety-free. But a focus on the future becomes a false god—a Janus-like forward-facing idol—when it stems from not trusting the one true God, who holds *all* things in His hands. Our fixation upon the future can distract us from the many vocations to which God even now is calling us.

Two Case Studies

THE FUTURE-DRIVEN STUDENT

Jordan entered his pastor's office with such excitement that the words streamed out of his mouth even before he sat down. He was ready—now. All had been made clear to him. Jordan *knew* God was now calling him to a great world-changing task, and he couldn't wait to tell his pastor about it. In rapid-fire and run-on sentences, Jordan feverishly explained that he had *finally* discovered his true vocation. Jordan would use his academic gifts for biology and chemistry, combine them with his love of people and God's Word, and establish a medical mission in a needy African country. God had recently placed upon his heart this one great calling, which Jordan would now seek after with all his heart—so he had come to believe.

Knowing this college-age student pretty well, the pastor calmly tried to affirm Jordan's excitement over this new calling while also offering some guidance and caution. Like a skilled surgeon, the pastor gently but precisely began to poke around Jordan's present activities, future plans, and understanding of vocation. As it turns out, ever since this big epiphany about what God wanted him to do, Jordan had grown neglectful of his studies, his relationships, and his faith. Other than those specific courses deemed useful to his future calling, he became lazy with his homework—why bother studying something with so little relevance to his life? Last week, he missed his mom's birthday and was pretty short with his roommate, but he spent endless hours online researching the medical needs of several African countries. It has created some tension with his girlfriend too. They've been serious for more than a year now, but Jordan has never once discussed how all this might affect their relationship and their future together. He misconstrues her quite understandable concerns as standing in opposition to God's work and calling on *his* life. Worse still, Jordan's preoccupation with what he feels God wants him to do in the future has wreaked havoc on his spiritual life. Simple acts of charity and kindness, daily Scripture reading, and even worship have taken a back seat to this one quest that, in Jordan's mind, is God's sole purpose for his life.

Jordan is mistaken in his unspoken assumption that there is only one great thing God has placed him on this earth to do. He has used the excuse of questing after it to neglect the many callings God presently asks him to fulfill: be a good student, love his mother, respect his roommate, be considerate to his girlfriend, grow in understanding of his baptismal grace, hear God's Word daily. Jordan is worshiping Janus because he obsesses over the future calling he's assigned himself while ignoring what God has given him to do today and every day. His future "calling" has disrupted his present callings.

Perhaps even more concerning, what happens if the great medical mission Jordan hopes to establish never comes to fruition? Does this mean he's a failure? Has he disappointed God and ignored His purposes? Did God mislead him or misdirect him? Will his life ever find full meaning and purpose? Jordan has failed to realize that *his calling in life should be seen in the present rather than the future.*

Ministering to people's physical needs while witnessing to Christ in a foreign country is, of course, a noble and God-pleasing goal. It is healthy to prayerfully consider how God might use us to do His work in the future. However, too often the evil one twists our self-discovered and self-appointed future callings, distracting us from tasks and relationships that are right in front of us. We follow Janus's gaze, obsessing over the future while ignoring the present.

The Future-Driving Parent

No one could question Grace's love for her eight-year-old daughter, Lexi. She would always be there for her, provide for her every need, and help shape her into a wonderful, successful human being. But Grace's love had recently become off-balanced because of Janus's constant forward-looking face. Lexi's ever-increasing activities had become mere preparation for future success, imposed upon her by a loving but overreaching mom. All the lessons, homework, after-school programs, and strict discipline had one goal: to create the most productive, successful, superstar child possible. Practice time and homework increased; play time and simply snuggling together on the couch decreased. Lexi sprinted off to one enriching and challenging activity after another, embracing the excitement of it all but secretly wondering if she could ever measure up. Grace's motivation certainly stemmed partially from love—any good parent wants her children to achieve their best and grow into flourishing young adults. But when completely honest with herself, Grace would discover some less-than altruistic reasons for pushing Lexi so hard.

It took a difficult and honest confrontation by a friend over a cup of coffee, some deep introspection and prayer, and a rather convicting sermon at church, but Grace came to an important realization about her relationship with her daughter. Lexi had been used to fulfill *Grace's* own unmet needs. Some of this stemmed from unresolved issues in Grace's own childhood—Lexi would be given every opportunity she hadn't been, find success where she hadn't, and be pushed in ways she wished she would have been. But most of it, quite honestly, was simply driven by pride: a beautiful, successful, talented, popular, overachieving daughter sure makes the mom look good!

Whatever the motivation, Grace decided to make some significant changes in both her attitude and her interactions with her daughter. She would obsess less about the future—who Lexi would become and how she should be shaped and driven for success—and rest more in the present. They cut out a few extracurriculars (Lexi was only doing ballet for her mom anyway). They went for leisurely walks together. They worked in the garden together and didn't worry so much about getting dirty. Sometimes they didn't really do anything in particular; just hung out, laughed, and played. The moment of confirmation came one Sunday afternoon during a messy brownie-baking date. Both giggling with chocolate on their noses, Lexi turned to her mom and said, "Mom, I love being with you. I wish we could just bake brownies together forever."

Grace smashed the false god Janus in her heart and life and turned in trust toward the one true God, who holds everything in His hands—past, present, and future. Nothing in her difficult past nor anything she thought her daughter was supposed to achieve could steal from them the sacred present. Their most important calling was now; it was not waiting for them in effort, achievement, and success. Grace had learned one of the most important lessons of the vocation of parenthood: what your children really want from you is *you*—present-tense moments of love, affection, and joy. On that day when you've departed from this world, they won't care how you drove them to success as much as how you sat with them, laughed, played, and loved.

> *I am the Alpha and the Omega, the first and the last, the beginning and the end.* (REVELATION 22:13)

Most of our life callings we already have, presently. Very few of them still await us. They all have sacred value, an importance beyond the world's standards of success or achievement, if we seek to fulfill them in response to God's grace and in love for those He's given us. Vocation is best understood in the plural *and* the present. We have calling*s* and we have them *now*. No doubt some important and life-altering tasks, responsibilities, and relationships will arise in the future: a college selected, a career path chosen, a spouse married, a retirement home purchased. But too often our obsession with discerning, determining, and manipulating the future distracts us from the simple, sacred things God has already given us to do.

Christ Jesus stands in all our doorways, at every mile marker, and with all our beginnings and endings. The arms of His eternal love stretch forth from the cross, ever backward and ever forward, bringing forgiveness, peace, and renewal. No past is too painful, no future too uncertain for His power and grace. Christians in faith know their Lord rules all things in heaven and earth, and thus cast aside the two-faced god of preoccupation with the past and fixation upon the future. In this freedom, their eyes open to the many sacred callings presently before them, and in love they seek to be extensions of God's gracious activity to those around them.

· ·

A PRAYER FOR STRENGTH IN OUR VOCATIONS

Make me present in Your presence, O God. Turn my untrusting eyes away from the gods of my past, which shackle me by shame and guilt. Refocus my sight not upon faithless fears of the future, but solely upon the work of Christ Jesus, whose wounds alone make all things new. By Your Spirit, give me new eyes that behold in those placed on my path a calling of love and service. Through Jesus Christ, our Lord. Amen.

· ·

Present Tense

Martin Luther's redefinition of vocation—which applied the concept to all good and godly work, relationships, and positions—has a remarkable emphasis on the present. His teaching on Confession in the Small Catechism concerning which sins Christians should confess encourages an examination of one's present stations in life:

> Consider your place in life according to the Ten Commandments: Are you are a father, mother, son, daughter, husband, wife, or worker? Have you been disobedient, unfaithful, or lazy? Have you been hot-tempered, rude, or quarrelsome? Have you hurt someone

by your words or deeds? Have you stolen, been negligent, wasted anything, or done any harm?[11]

The vast majority of the population in Luther's day had limited mobility and little choice about their work. Born in a certain region and into a specific family and most likely an occupation, most people remained *where* they were, doing *what* had been given them. Although a growing bourgeois class opened up opportunities for some in the sixteenth century, most stations in life remained remarkably static.

In contrast, choice in our world has grown exponentially. This, of course, comes with many benefits. You can travel across the country to choose a college that fits your needs; your children aren't restrained to do the same job as you; they don't even have to live near you, and you can still keep in touch. People can much more easily change jobs, retrain, reeducate, or relocate.

Despite these obvious benefits, the truth remains that most of our callings are unfolding right now. They are present-tense callings. We've each already been given many tasks to accomplish, responsibilities to discharge, people with whom we relate, and places we live, work, study, and play. Indeed, too often the quest to discover that one great future calling of God distracts us from what He's already given us. In his commentary on the Book of Genesis, Martin Luther took note of Abraham and Sarah's servile care in feeding and waiting upon the three visitors of chapter 18. They cheerfully and diligently gather food, prepare dinner, and serve their guests in the most menial way. Applying this to the idea of vocation, Luther underscored the common, earthly, everyday callings God places before us:

> If you are a student, mind your studies; if you are a maid, sweep the house; if you are a servant, care for the horses, etc. A monk may live a harder life, wear poorer clothes, but he will never be truly able to say

---

11   Small Catechism, Confession.

that he serves God in this manner. But they who serve society, the state, and the church can say it.[12]

Present-Tense Blessings

God bestows countless blessings upon those who live present-tense lives. Not least of these is an *awareness* that He, through His grace, is already at work through us. When the word of Christ awakens us to God's current activity in our lives, we find our value not in possible future accomplishments or achievements—some of which may never come—but simply in God's grace *for us* and then *through us*. Christ Jesus lives through us *now*. No one has to wait to begin a life of love and service.

Another blessing comes in finding *joy* in the smallest daily service. You don't have to have your whole life figured out, or plot a perfect path into the future, or select the best major or most meaningful job, or wait until that "one day" when God begins to work. Our callings are already here. God is fully engaged in the smallest things unfolding—today. The knowledge that God, the Creator of the universe, chooses to extend His providential care through *us* in the simplest and humblest activities of daily life brings great joy indeed!

It similarly leads to great *contentment*. If you mistakenly consider "calling" to be mainly about a future work or accomplishment, a tremendous amount of anxiety can follow. What if you never discover your calling? How do you know when you've achieved it? What if it's not as fun or dramatic as anticipated? What's the best way to discern it? How will you know for sure when you do? In contrast, when you realize that at this very moment you've already been given most of what you're called to do in life, it's easy to get busy serving the faces, places, and spaces of life (see chapter 1). You can be free from the incredible pressure of having to discover the one great future calling

---

12   Trans. from George W. Forell, *Faith Active in Love* (Minneapolis: Augsburg, 1964), 148. WA (Weimar Edition) xlii, 30, 31; originally cited in Kurt K. Hendel's unpublished essay, "Vocation: A Lutheran Understanding," 8–9. Used by permission. Cf. LW 3:218.

and be free from guilt or disappointment when it seems you haven't found it or accomplished it.

Finally, living a present-tense life brings the blessing of *valuing others* in who they are, not just in what they accomplish. Just as God has given you most of your callings, currently, in the present, the same is true of those around you. Their identity does not stem from how many souls they might save once they're a pastor or missionary; or what great job they'll land after they graduate from college; or whether they establish a world-changing nonprofit company one day; or whom they might marry, where they might live, and how much money they'll make. Because of the work of Christ Jesus—and *solely* because of His work—the people in your life do not simply have potential value. They have *full value* right now, as forgiven and redeemed children of God. Their *present* matters, and their *presence* matters.

Living Present Tense

When he became aware of the many vocations God had placed in his life, present tense, Josh felt like the eyes of his heart opened (Ephesians 1:18). He started to take seriously not just the desire to serve in youth ministry at a church one day but the tasks, relationships, and responsibilities God had already given him. Being a good student didn't just mean attentiveness to courses he found interesting or applicable. The people in his life were no longer simply tools to help him achieve his dreams. Josh began applying himself with diligence to the seemingly insignificant tasks of cleaning the bathroom, shoveling the neighbor's driveway, greeting a co-worker with warmth, and babysitting his little brother. Josh understood these callings to have value because God had given them, so he was to exercise them in faith. He started living present tense.

Kirsten's anxiety began to melt away. As a stay-at-home mom overseeing three small children and their development, it was easy to add constant pressure to herself . . . and her children. She used to expend endless energy obsessing about the many things necessary to prepare her children for the great future she'd planned for them.

But then Kirsten learned to relax a bit about all the kids' activities and accomplishments. She learned to savor the sacred moments and know the day-to-day joys of motherhood. She started living present tense.

Ana lived in an incessant stress of trying to discern God's plans for her life. She had many talents—academic, social, and organizational—but also deeply desired to be a wife and mother one day. The sometimes conflicting callings of education, career, professional advancement, service, and ministry—along with the dream of a family—seemed overwhelming. But by God's grace, Ana came to truly trust that all will unfold according to God's perfect plan. As much as Christ loved her at Calvary, He loved her still and would guide her into the future. Ana was at peace knowing that God had given her enough to do just for today. She realized that the majority of her callings wouldn't change regardless of her career and family choices. She started living present tense.

Drowning Janus

When Christians speak of Baptism, they often employ the most positive and even flowery of words: *wonder, amazement, joy, celebration, beauty, life, light, peace.* How appropriate are such words, given the blessings of Baptism, which brings us into the kingdom of God! There is, however, a dark and even violent side to Baptism—spiritually speaking, that is. When applied to our old sinful selves (the old Adam in each of us), a whole list of less, shall we say, optimistic terms comes to mind: *death, drowning, destruction, violence, struggle, killing.* Such language is equally appropriate and even necessary because so long as we remain in these bodies this side of Christ's return, sin still affects us and infects us. Our old sinful self—that broken, fallen, and rebellious nature—clings with all its evil energy to us, dragging us back to sin and away from Christ. Through daily repentance and remembrance of our Baptism, the old self is put away, drowned. The old Adam must die through true acknowledgment and confession of sin.

St. Paul understood this, which is why in his great chapter on Baptism (Romans 6) he doesn't shy away from rather morbid language.

Making the case that forgiven sinners, as new creatures, leave behind their old ways, St. Paul uses some form of the word *dead* fourteen times in just eleven verses. Baptism does bring new life, but it does so only because it first brings new death. We are grafted into the life, death, and resurrection of Jesus Christ, our old selves being killed and our new selves coming forth to love and serve in resurrection power:

> For if we have been united with Him in a death like His, we shall certainly be united with Him in a resurrection like His. We know that our old self was crucified with Him in order that the body of sin might be brought to nothing, so that we would no longer be enslaved to sin. For one who has died has been set free from sin. Now if we have died with Christ, we believe that we will also live with Him. We know that Christ, being raised from the dead, will never die again; death no longer has dominion over Him. For the death He died He died to sin, once for all, but the life He lives He lives to God. So you also must consider yourselves dead to sin and alive to God in Christ Jesus. (ROMANS 6:5–11)

The old sinful self doesn't go down easy either. It will push back, fight, scratch, resurface, and resurge throughout our earthly journey. Christians are especially aware of and weary of this constant battle. Again, even the great St. Paul described with exasperation his constant struggle with sin:

> For I know that nothing good dwells in me, that is, in my flesh. For I have the desire to do what is right, but not the ability to carry it out. For I do not do the good I want, but the evil I do not want is what I keep on doing. . . . So I find it to be a law that when I want to do right, evil lies close at hand. . . . Wretched man that I am! Who will deliver me from this body of

death? Thanks be to God through Jesus Christ our Lord! (ROMANS 7:18–19, 21, 24–25)

This is why remembering our Baptism remains a constant, lifelong imperative. We return to our Baptism through both repentance and faith. Repentance is a spiritually violent act. We hate sin, turn from it, kill it off in our lives, stick our old selves in the grave, bury the old Adam six feet under. Anyone who's ever struggled with sin—or had their sin exposed before others—knows the violence of this "spiritual homicide" of the old Adam. Faith, on the other hand, knows, believes, trusts, and rests assured that because we remain united with the person and work of Christ Jesus through Baptism, our eternal security and salvation cannot be in doubt.

Martin Luther didn't shy away from graphic language when describing what happens in Baptism. One of his favorite images was of an intentional drowning—certainly not the most positive description, but fitting nonetheless:

> *What does such baptizing with water indicate?* It indicates that the Old Adam in us should by daily contrition and repentance be drowned and die with all sins and evil desires, and that a new man should daily emerge and arise to live before God in righteousness and purity forever.[13]

---

13   Small Catechism, Baptism, Fourth Part.

These two parts, (a) to be sunk under the water and (b) drawn out again, signify Baptism's power and work. It is nothing other than putting to death the old Adam and affecting the new man's resurrection. . . . Both of these things must take place in us all our lives.

LARGE CATECHISM, PART 4, PARAGRAPH 65

The false god Janus won't go down easily either. He stares incessantly into the past, fixating so much on our previous sin, shame, and shortcomings—although they all are forgiven in Christ—that we would deny the Gospel, refuse to move forward in faith and love, and eventually even despair of God's grace. Conversely, his forward-looking gaze enslaves us to fear, worry, and anxiety, causing us to mistrust Christ, the one who forged time and space and holds all things in His hands. Janus needs to be drowned, put down, buried six feet under through repentance and faith. This happens when we acknowledge the sinful effects of this false god in our lives, turn away from its deception, and focus our eyes firmly on Jesus, the author and perfecter of our faith (Hebrews 12:2).

Holy Baptism is the essential and foundational calling of every Christian. It is the source from which all other godly vocations spring. Our baptismal calling is *past tense.* Through it, God grafts us into the life, death, and resurrection of Jesus Christ. What occurred more than two thousand years ago—long before any of us and apart from our efforts or activity—becomes fully ours through faith. Our baptismal calling is *present tense.* The source of our identity, security, and meaning comes not from our accomplishments or achievements, power or prestige, fame or fortune, but solely from whom we have been made in Christ Jesus.[14] Resting in His presence, we can rest in the present, confident that He who began this good work will bring it to completion at the day of Jesus Christ (Philippians 1:6). Our baptismal calling is *future tense*. Because I know the One who holds the future—who rules enthroned above time and space, above all kingdoms, powers, and princes—I can be at peace concerning what is to come. No failure, no task, no tragedy, not even death itself can separate me from His love. What worries can outweigh His love? What anxieties speak louder than His eternal voice? Being connected to Christ through Baptism means the gift of ultimate, eternal peace. I will one day be with Him forever, beyond all sin, suffering, sickness, or stress, rejoicing eternally in His unending *presence*.

A PRAYER FOR HELP ON LIFE'S JOURNEY

Blessed are all Your saints, O God and King, who have traveled over the tempestuous sea of this mortal life, and have made the harbor of peace and happiness. Watch over us who are still in our dangerous voyage, and remember such as lie exposed to the rough storms of trouble and temptations. Frail is our vessel, and the ocean is wide; but as in Your mercy You have set our course, so steer the vessel of our life toward the everlasting shore of peace. Bring us at length to the quiet haven of our heart's desire, where You, O our God, are blessed, and live and reign forever and ever. Amen. ST. AUGUSTINE, ATTR.

---

14   The categories of identity, security, and meaning are drawn from Robert Kolb, *Speaking the Gospel Today: A Theology for Evangelism* (St. Louis: CPH, 1984), 19.

For Discussion

1. How is Martin Luther's explanation of the First Commandment helpful but also convicting (page 32)?

2. Describe a time in your life when your obsession with the past became problematic or even idolatrous.

3. How was Aaron's inability to be free of the past hindering his future (pages 32–33)?

4. What's the definition of "repristination," and how might this be detrimental to a congregation, school, or organization (page 35)? Have you ever been in a situation where you felt the past was ruining the future?

5. In what ways can anxiety about the future be a false god (pages 37–38)?

6. Share a time when your fixation on the future caused you to neglect a present calling.

7. What are some of the dangerous results of parents trying to live through their children (page 41)?

8. If you have children, discuss the challenge of wanting to prepare your kids for the future while also enjoying the present.

9. How did Grace get off balance in her parenting of Lexi (pages 40–42)?

10. Which character trying to live present tense can you most relate to (pages 46–47)?

11. What changes might you hope to make in order to better live "present tense"?

12. "Repentance is a spiritually violent act" (page 49). What does this mean?

CHAPTER 3

DIAPERS AND SIPPY CUPS

Our calling in life is better understood in the ordinary rather than the dramatic.

We all want to make a difference, move mountains by faith, slay Goliaths with but five small stones, and leave a legacy of love and service. When we come to understand the depths and the power of Christ's love, Christians feel compelled to take that faith into action in both word and deed. The Lutheran tradition, in particular, boasts world-altering all-stars whose lives of faith dramatically impacted humanity or even altered history. If the Church operated like a sports team, these would be the saints whose numbers are retired and jerseys hung somewhere high on the sanctuary walls.

Martin Luther (1483–1546) is a good place to start. His recovery of the Christian Gospel for the Church and the reforms that flowed from his study of the Scriptures mark him as one of the most significant historical figures of all time. The changes unleashed by his challenge to spiritual and temporal authority altered religion, politics, culture, and the social fabric of Europe for centuries. Luther's three-fold emphasis of grace alone (*sola gratia*), faith alone (*sola fides*), and Scripture alone (*sola scriptura*) taught that each individual person has direct access to God's grace by believing in the saving work of Jesus

Christ as revealed in the Bible. Salvation is *received*, not *achieved*, and this is not of ourselves, it is a gift of God.

> *For by grace you have been saved through faith. And this is not your own doing; it is the gift of God, not a result of works, so that no one may boast.* (EPHESIANS 2:8–9)

The imperatives of these spiritual insights brought about new art forms, new written languages, and new educational approaches that are still with us today. Even the words we speak and the way we learn language trace their roots to the Reformation. What is more, the geopolitical map of Europe was redrawn because of Luther's Reformation, entire nations and empires casting themselves as Protestant or Catholic and fighting wars over their religious identity. The social changes stemming from Luther's insights are often underappreciated by today's historians. The modern concepts of public education, civil marriage licenses, and even state-funded welfare first arose in Protestant Germany and affect millions of lives daily. Lastly, as we have seen, Martin Luther's transformation of the concept of vocation—expanding it to all godly and useful roles fulfilled in the church, government, home, or workplace—brought incalculable social change throughout the Western world.

Another historical all-star whose number we might retire is Dietrich Bonhoeffer (1906–45). Born into a German family that fostered creativity and critical thinking, Bonhoeffer established himself at an early age as one who just wouldn't follow the crowd. Much to the disappointment of his overachieving parents, he chose to study theology and follow the calling to be a theologian and Lutheran pastor. During his postgraduate fellowship, while overseas at Union Seminary in New York, Bonhoeffer had a spiritual awakening while experiencing the fervor of faith in African American churches in the United

States. After the rise of Nazism in Germany, Bonhoeffer returned from safety in the US to resist Hitler's intrusion and corruption of the Christian Church. Publishing against the Nazi program, leading an underground seminary, rescuing Jews out of Germany, working as a double agent, and eventually (and controversially) joining in the plot to assassinate Hitler fills out the resume of this remarkable and inspirational figure. His final days were spent in a Nazi concentration camp. Bonhoeffer was hung naked at Flossenbürg days before the camp was liberated by the Allied forces. An eyewitness remarked on the peace and confidence of Bonhoeffer's fervent prayer before his execution.[15]

You've heard of Rosa Parks—the Montgomery civil rights leader whose refusal to give up her seat to a white passenger helped spark the challenge to Alabama's segregation laws. But you may not have heard of Rosa Young (1890–1971)—the "Second Rosa"—whose Christian faith inspired her to bring education and the Gospel to the rural poor of central Alabama. As an African American woman, Rosa Young fought the battle against injustice on three fronts: racism, sexism, and the plight of the uneducated and impoverished in rural America. Inspired by the Lutheran vision of parochial education, she worked tirelessly to establish congregational schools throughout Alabama, uplifting the faith and lives of thousands for whom education had previously only been a dream. "Rosa Young's ministry singlehandedly brought the Lutheran church to rural Alabama and led to the founding of the only historically black Lutheran college in the nation."[16]

....

15   Eric Metaxas, *Bonhoeffer: Pastor, Martyr, Prophet, Spy* (Nashville: Thomas Nelson, 2010), 528.

16   Christine S. Weerts, "St. Rosa Young," *Lutheran Forum* 43, no. 2 (Summer 2009), 33, accessed December 19, 2019, https://www.lutheranforum.com/blog/st-rosa-young.

"He that is greatest among you shall be your servant," is the language of the Great Teacher. To serve is regarded as a divine privilege as well as a duty by every right-minded man. Do something worthy for mankind, is the cry of the civilized world. Give light to those who are in darkness; sustain the weak and faltering; befriend and aid the poor and needy. . . . As we go from these university halls into the battle of life, where our work is to be done and our places among men to be decided, we should go in the spirit of service, with a determination to do all in our power to uplift humanity. . . . People are looking to us for strength and help. They need our best efforts, our bravest words, our noblest deeds, our tenderest love, and our most helpful sympathy. This is a needy world; outstretched hands may be seen by the thousands asking for aid. It is our duty to relieve human wants. Let us place our standard high, but be willing to do the lowest task, the most distasteful labor, be ever helpful and generous, and be ready to lend a helping hand. Good service is an unfailing guide to success. There is nothing more reputable to a race or nation than Christian service. So let us not hesitate, but grasp every opportunity that will enable us to do some good for others.[17]

ROSA YOUNG

17   Rosa J. Young, *Light in the Dark Belt* (St. Louis: Concordia Publishing House, 1950), 40–42.

A fourth all-star from the Church Triumphant team followed in the path of Dietrich Bonhoeffer, sacrificing his life for his Christian convictions. Gudina Tumsa (1929–79) served as general secretary of the Lutheran Church in Ethiopia, the Ethiopian Evangelical Church Mekane Yesus (Place of Jesus). Tumsa's work combined a clear understanding of the Gospel with the desire for holistic ministry among Africa's poorest minorities. When the Marxist revolution arose in Ethiopia in the early 1970s, the church's theology, mission, and witness came under direct attack. The brutal persecution of Ethiopian faith leaders during the 1970s remains one of the most underappreciated stories of twentieth-century Christian martyrdom. Tumsa himself refused to merge either the church's teachings or his personal convictions into any governmental system or earthly ideology. Rather than compromise the truth of the Gospel or abandon his call and his people, Tumsa chose to stay and preach, regardless of the consequences. Persecuted, tortured, and finally abducted and executed, Tumsa's legacy is one of a deep faith in Jesus, a life of piety and sacrifice, and an unwavering conviction concerning the truth of the Gospel. The Place of Jesus is now the largest Lutheran church body in Africa. Days before his martyrdom, Tumsa wrote about sacrifice and service in the name of Christ:

> As someone has said, when a person is called to follow Christ, that person is called to die. It means a redirection of the purpose of life, that is death to one's own wishes and personal desires and finding the greatest satisfaction in living for and serving the one who died for us and was raised from death (2 Corinthians 5:13, 14). . . .

> A responsible Christian does not aggravate any situation and thereby court martyrdom. . . . to be a Christian is not to be a hero to make history for oneself. A Christian goes as a lamb to be slaughtered only

when he/she knows that this is in complete accord with the will of God who has called him to his service.[18]

These examples from the Lutheran tradition both inspire and edify us—we can see the dramatic ways God worked His purposes through people. All-stars like Luther, Bonhoeffer, Young, and Tumsa fill us with thanksgiving and praise to God for their witness, faith, and lives of service and sacrifice. Arguably the most remarkable thing about them, however, is that not one of them actually set out to do anything dramatic or world-changing for God. In each case, they simply began by being faithful in the everyday, ordinary callings God had placed upon their lives. Not one of them would have or could have predicted being included on a list of saints who have impacted or inspired millions through great personal sacrifice. They never dreamed of having their numbers retired, so to speak. Rather, each of them began with being faithful in the smallest, seemingly insignificant callings, which God then transformed into a lasting legacy of world-changing proportions.

Martin Luther didn't even want to study theology, initially. If he had followed his father's designs, he would have stuck with law, made better money, and left theology to others. Until the posting of his Ninety-Five Theses on October 31, 1517, he remained an obscure Augustinian monk and university lecturer. Others printed, translated, and widely disseminated Luther's now-famous theses—he had no intention of starting a reformation and certainly never dreamed of personally opposing the sacred and secular rulers of Europe. The subsequent controversy over Luther's provocative words—and indeed the personal turmoil that arose because of the controversy—dragged him back into the Word of God in a quest for truth, certainty, and grace. He never once set out to do something dramatic for God and change the world. Rather, his callings as a priest, scholar, and baptized

---

18   Gudina Tumsa, *Witness and Discipleship: Leadership of the Church in Multi-Ethnic Ethiopia in a Time of Revolution* (Addis Ababa, Ethiopia: Gudina Tumsa Foundation, 2003), 11–12. Cited in Darrell Jodock, "Gudina Tumsa awarded the Christus Lux Mundi," Story Magazine (Third Quarter: 2004), Luther Seminary, St. Paul.

Christian compelled him to study the Word, seek the truth, and proclaim that truth boldly in the face of opposition. Faithfulness in the ordinary, everyday callings of life—"sweating the small stuff," so to speak—is the beginning of any great task and a virtue of any great person.

· ·

The first of Luther's Ninety Five Theses: When our Lord and Master Jesus Christ said, "Repent," He willed the entire life of believers to be one of repentance. LW 31:25

· ·

The same could be said of our other all-star players described above. Dietrich Bonhoeffer most certainly did not choose to study theology in order to oppose the twentieth century's cruelest despot. Hitler's rise to power would come a decade later. Rather, Bonhoeffer's clear understanding of the theology of the cross and his faithfulness to following only Jesus would make any casual compromise impossible once the Nazi takeover began. Rosa Young began with the simple, plain needs of those in her community—the faces she encountered in the impoverished Jim Crow South. These children needed Jesus, and they needed education. Young simply began there, and not with a grandiose plan to educate thousands, found a college, and bring social and religious change to Alabama. Gudina Tumsa had no idea that the communist revolution would come to Ethiopia or that its doctrines would oppose so fiercely the Christian Gospel. His faithfulness to his Lord began in the most unassuming places—his Bible, his study, the homes of his people, his calling as a pastor, and the needs of the sheep God brought to him.

None of us can predict or control the chances and changes of life, and very few of us will ever have our names listed alongside saints like these. Yet we are called to be faithful in the smallest *and* the largest of callings. God sees our "sweating the small stuff," and He will work through us according to His will, for His purposes, and in His time.

> *One who is faithful in a very little is also faithful in much, and one who is dishonest in a very little is also dishonest in much.* (LUKE 16:10)

A PRAYER OF GOOD COURAGE

Lord God, You have called Your servants to ventures of which we cannot see the ending, by paths as yet untrodden, through perils unknown. Give us faith to go out with good courage, not knowing where we go but only that Your hand is leading us and Your love supporting us; through Jesus Christ, our Lord. Amen. *LSB*, PAGE 311

Sweating the Small Stuff

Abigail *knew* that God had big plans for her. During high school, she went with her youth group on a short-term mission trip to Guatemala, and the experience changed her life. She learned about herself—that God had given her gifts to use in service toward others *and* that she actually enjoyed using those gifts. She learned about others—the breadth of the Christian witness throughout the world and the inspiring faith of brothers and sisters in an impoverished country who have so little but rejoice always. She learned about her future. Abigail's powerful experiences on that ten-day mission trip—daily immersed in God's Word, fellowshiping with other believers, selflessly serving the needy, and bringing them Jesus—all moved her to consider pursuing professional church work as a career.

A couple of months after returning from Guatemala, Abigail decided to sit down with her youth director and discuss her future dreams. Matt had served at their church for more than ten years and knew that the powerful emotions young people experience during these trips need the guidance of wisdom and moderation. Matt talked with Abigail and her parents over lunch. While encouraging her dreams and validating God's prompting in her life, he gave them the best advice they could have received. "Start with the small stuff," Matt counseled. "Be faithful with the little, daily, often mundane tasks God gives, and He'll get you where you need to be."

Abigail took this to heart. She stayed active in her youth group, helped around the house and especially with her younger siblings, immersed herself in God's Word and in prayer, got active in her community, and remained conscientious in school and with her part-time job. The good news is that she did, in the end, decide to go into full-time, professional service in the Church. Inspired by her work with the children of Guatemala, Abigail went to a Lutheran university to study education. She completed her student teaching overseas, received a call to an urban school, and has plans to one day work for a large nonprofit that sponsors an orphanage. Her youth director did not dismiss her dreams, but he did remind her that *our calling in life is best understood in the ordinary rather than the dramatic.* The big stuff *may* come according to God's plan and timing, but the little stuff *will* certainly always be there. By "sweating the small stuff"—that is, by taking seriously the commonplace callings of family, school, and community—Abigail was fulfilling Christ's law of love while also preparing herself for what God might unfold for her in the future.

> *His master said to him, "Well done, good and faithful servant. You have been faithful over a little; I will set you over much. Enter into the joy of your master."* (MATTHEW 25:23)

Jayla had grown discouraged and even depressed. The moment of crisis came on a hectic weekend when her husband, Elijah, was out of town for work. Elijah was a good man and a great husband and father. A couple of times a year, his company needed him to go out of state for a long weekend of presentations. This was part of the deal—they both knew it—and they had decided together that the income and opportunity would be worth the sacrifice of his time away from her and their kids. In the middle of a survival weekend of dirty diapers, spilled sippy cups, and potty training, Jayla melted down in tears. The issue wasn't so much that she couldn't handle being a mother of three kids, all under the age of 5—although no one doubts the challenges involved. She managed with competence and grace the unending stress and endless tasks of modern motherhood. Rather, her own dismissive attitude toward the mundane callings preoccupying her life kept dragging her ever downward.

It wasn't supposed to be this way, you see. Her present life had not lived up to the "high calling of God" she and others expected for her. Cleaning up poopy bottoms, tossing Goldfish snacks and granola bars into a diaper bag, packing a minimum of two lunches per day before 7:30 a.m., and making sure the floor wasn't completely covered in toys were not awe-inspiring achievements in her mind. If she happened to run into one of her high school teachers at the grocery store or chat with her college roommate online, embarrassment and even shame would take over. What was she supposed to say when they would ask, "So . . . what are you doing with your life these days?" "I'm knee-deep in diapers and sippy cups" would be the honest response. Or "just trying to make it to nap time." Jayla felt that she was meant for more and sensed disappointment when those she admired found out she hadn't gone to grad school, solved world hunger, or won a Nobel Prize. She was "just" a mom, and at times not even a very good one. Her expectations of greatness came crashing down on her that weekend. She loved her family but couldn't love herself while mired in the mundane.

On Sunday morning, Jayla didn't even manage to pull things together enough to get the kids to church—yet another reason to beat herself up. A "white-flag . . . I surrender!" morning meant sugared cereal for the kids, unlimited screen time, and wearing pajamas until noon. Finally mustering the energy to retrieve Friday's snail mail, Jayla found an envelope decorated in her favorite color—turquoise blue. She sat with the baby on her lap and read the letter aloud:

Dear Jayla,

My child. Your mundane moments matter to Me. They are filled with eternal significance, even when they seem unimportant by this world's standards. You're right: you probably won't receive a community service award or an honorary doctorate for potty training your kids. But you need to know that these basic, thankless tasks have My breath of life in them. I am at work *through* you: your hands are My hands; your labors, Mine; your heart, even, Mine. Do not be discouraged. Lift up your eyes of faith. Know that when I said, "I am with you," I meant it in the most real, down-to-earth, everyday way possible. I want you to fulfill these commonplace callings for a season, for now, and I promise that I mark these moments and see them for what they are—love and service to your family done in My name. I have no greater or more important purpose for you to fulfill right now than faithfulness amid the ordinary. It is I who call you to this, and I will remain with you through it all.

—Your Lord, Immanuel, God with Us

The handwriting was unmistakably Elijah's, but Jayla already knew the author. This was just like her husband—thinking ahead and mailing a thoughtful, creative note of encouragement before leaving town. He did recognize both the difficulty and the importance of her present callings—piles of laundry, nursing babies, playing with blocks. What was more, Elijah recognized that Jayla was certainly capable of the "much more" of this world's expectations. He married a woman every bit as talented and driven as he. He hoped that she knew how much he appreciated her and—even more—that she knew he saw God at work through her in the lives of their children.

Golden and Noble Works

Martin Luther's insights regarding vocation located the work of God, the highest of callings, in the daily, humdrum, not-so-dramatic roles, relationships, and responsibilities of regular life. He turned the question away from "How dramatic, super-spiritual, and world-changing is this activity?" to "Am I doing this in response to God's love and in service to my neighbor?" For Luther, the standard of evaluation became not so much what I do or accomplish but what I do with what God has given me.

The late medieval world considered the ordinary activities of marriage and family, house and home as lower activities—necessary, but mired in the muck of worldliness. In a treatise titled *The Estate of Marriage* (1522), Luther defends the everyday activities of family and farm, extolling these callings as higher and more useful even than the vows of celibacy practiced in the monastic orders. In response to those who would mock and denigrate the holy vocations of home and family, Luther writes:

What then does Christian faith say to this? It opens its eyes, looks upon all these insignificant, distasteful, and despised duties in the Spirit, and is aware that they are all adorned with divine approval as with the costliest gold and jewels.[19]

He equally encourages wives and husbands to rejoice in the value of their everyday activities. "A wife too should regard her duties in the same light, as she suckles the child, rocks and bathes it, and cares for it in other ways. . . . These are truly golden and noble works."[20]

On the other hand, Luther rebukes those who would ridicule the common tasks of parenting as beneath them or as lesser callings. Indeed, God smiles upon any commonplace activity done in His name and in service to others:

> Now you tell me, when a father goes ahead and washes diapers or performs some other mean task for his child, and someone ridicules him as an effeminate fool—though that father is acting in the spirit just described and in Christian faith—my dear fellow you tell me, which of the two is most keenly ridiculing the other? God, with all His angels and creatures, is smiling—not because that father is washing diapers, but because he is doing so in Christian faith.[21]

Our callings begin in the ordinary. When done in faith, as a way of honoring God and serving those He's placed before us, the lowliest tasks receive the highest praise: no diaper too stinky, no stack of dishes too overwhelming, no hamper of laundry too heavy. God smiles upon the commonplace with the same brightness as the noble and remarkable acts of the sainted all-stars. Christians begin their

19   LW 45:39.
20   LW 45:40.
21   LW 45:40.

discernment of God's high purposes for them in the everyday—by sweating the small stuff.

• •

Luther's insight, that one serves God by doing the sort of works that our various places in life require of us, made love exceedingly concrete. It took love out of so-called spiritual areas and related it to service to one's neighbor in what seemed very ordinary ways: raising children, caring for elderly parents, farming, participating in government, paying taxes, going to school. Every Christian, from the least to the greatest, from the youngest to the oldest, could now be seen to have a divine calling. This was the case because God creates and sustains the world that we sometimes call "ordinary," and God wants to see to it that this world is cared for and therefore calls each one of us to be involved in such care.[22]

• •

Gloves of God

God works through people. We probably wish this wasn't the case, most of the time, given how often we tend to mess things up. And certainly it's more exciting to look for the direct and dramatic interventions of God into human affairs—an epiphany telling you what to do, a miracle hitting you out of the blue, a windfall inheritance from a long-lost rich uncle. But for the vast majority of human history, God chooses to extend His providential hand into our lives through

....

22   Marc Kolden, *Christian's Calling in the World* (St. Paul: Centered Life, 2002), 8–9.

ordinary people . . . through *sinful*, ordinary people. We are the means, the conduits through which He provides for, protects, cares for, and loves His creation.

Martin Luther had a curious but helpful way of talking about this. He described people doing God's work as His masks—*Larvae Dei* (masks of God) is the Latin phrase. That is, although it seems like us on the outside, in reality God is behind it all. We're concealing His work, so to speak. God remains hidden behind the good we're doing in and for His creation. From the world's perspective, *we* plant food, drive trucks, patrol streets, teach children, coach teams, run businesses, create music, and construct highways. The eyes of faith, however, see God's activity behind it all. Through the farmer, *God* provides; through the truck driver, *God* delivers; through the police officer, *God* protects; through the teacher, *God* educates; through the musician, *God* inspires. We're His masks, giving the appearance that it's merely human beings at work. But remove our faces from the picture, and you'll behold God active in the world.

Lutheran pastor and scholar Robert Kolb offers a helpful summary of this teaching:

> Luther transformed the use of the word "calling" or "vocation" by assigning it to all Christians. Believers recognize that God has placed them in the structures of human life created by God and has called them to the tasks of caring for their creatures, human or otherwise, as agents of God's providential presence and care. Luther called people in the exercise of their response-abilities "masks of God," through whom God, for example, milks cows so that his human creatures may be nourished.[23]

---

23 Robert Kolb, "Called to Milk Cows and Govern Kingdoms: Martin Luther's Teaching on the Christian's Vocations," *Concordia Journal* (Spring 2013): 135.

Another helpful way of thinking about God's hidden but providential care active through people is to imagine that we are His gloves—the gloves of God. A doctor performs surgery, a nurse takes a temperature, a classmate extends a helpful hand, a friend offers comfort, a mom puts on a bandage, a relative lends money. In each of these cases, the outside world sees human hands, but the eyes of faith perceive a deeper reality. We are but the gloves of God concealing the divine reality, remaining on the surface as an external and outward appearance. God truly works in, through, and behind us to provide, preserve, order, direct, and care for His broken creation.

. . . .

This, then, is the great glory with which the Divine Majesty honors us: It works through us in such a manner that It says that our words are Its words and that our actions are Its actions, so that one can truthfully say that the mouth of a godly teacher is God's mouth and that the hand which you extend to alleviate the want of a brother is God's hand.

MARTIN LUTHER, LW 3:272

. . . .

Christian Gloves

Two important distinctions should be made in applying the idea of God's gloves to an understanding of vocation. The first pertains to the role of Christians and non-Christians who equally serve as God's gloves. The nonbelieving farmer raises equally good corn. The agnostic physician might be even more skilled and educated than a Christian one. Some of history's greatest composers, whose music inspires and brings joy to generations, rejected God. When your house is burning, you probably don't stop the firefighter to check his religious affiliation. Even with regard to our politicians, just because a candidate claims to believe in Jesus doesn't mean that he or she possesses the character, competence, experience, or salient ideas to govern wisely and equitably. All people—regardless of their religious background or their moral makeup—function as God's gloves in the world. As we shall see, however, Christians recognize and rejoice in this role, seeking God's will in their service while striving to be the best masks, the greatest gloves they can be, to His glory.

Four touchstones distinguish Christians and non-Christians who serve as extensions of God's providential care in society: motive, mood, manner, and mission.

The *motive* of a Christian is not selfishness or pride, how much money one can make, or how prominent and admirable an occupation might be. Rather, understanding the eternal Gospel of God's graciousness on the cross, the baptized believer seeks to respond to God's great love by being His instrument in love and service to others. Christians remain engaged in the world because God made it, redeemed it, and will one day restore it. They recognize that God the Holy Spirit has endowed them with gifts—knowledge, skills, resources, opportunities, time, talents, treasures—which are to be stewarded in helpful ways for the good of the world and the Church. And if they come into financial gain or earthly advancement and prestige, they glorify God, bear witness to the hope that is within them, and bless others with what God has given them.

The *mood* of the Christian contrasts sharply with others who function as God's gloves. Both cheerfulness and confidence flow from a heart that knows the Gospel. In their work amid the structures of society—roles, relationships, and responsibilities—a baptized child of God rejoices in the knowledge that God indeed works through them for others. What a mysterious privilege, to be the gloves of God! The Creator of the universe, God Almighty Himself, moves through me in planting, protecting, providing, healing, teaching, inspiring, buying, selling, leading, and governing. The nonbeliever, on the other hand, discerns nothing greater or more important going on other than the tasks and activities immediately at hand. He or she might be doing good things, and certainly God works equally through them for others, but no awe, amazement, or thanksgiving flows from his or her work. The mood of the Christian is likewise filled with confidence. If indeed God remains active in, through, and behind me, I can be assured that my work has sacred purpose and value, having received His blessing. No task is too menial, no relationship too trivial, no project too complex, no challenge too daunting since God stands behind it all.

In contrast to others, the Christian, in recognizing his or her role as the gloves of God, seeks to grow in both skill and virtue in the carrying out of this work. God both deserves and demands the best from His masks and gloves. If they were not His, He would not be the least concerned. But since they *are*, both their effectiveness and integrity matters. Christians, then, strive to grow in their skills and usefulness, as well as in the character of their sanctified lives expressed in the world around them. They do this precisely because God moves through their work. They represent Him and work for Him. Embracing this role as God's agents, the *manner* through which Christians fulfill their responsibilities is markedly different. How they conduct themselves, the ways they express their faith, the integrity they display, the fervor that accompanies their work all stem from the knowledge that God labors in their labors.

Not so with the nonbeliever. The businessman might as well skim a bit off the top; the doctor revel in her own power; the successful trader hoard his money; the famous athlete flaunt her success; the politician lie to win an election; the musician produce whatever sells, no matter the moral or societal consequences. Christians, too, will sin in the exercise of their vocations. So long as we remain in our fallen bodies in a fallen world, no job, activity, or role will reach perfection. This is also why Christians, in contrast to their nonbelieving co-workers and friends, return continuously to Christ's Word and Sacraments for redemption and renewal. Being God's gloves is tough business—even overwhelming at times. All the more reason to continually return to the one, unending source of strength and forgiveness.

> *Finally, brothers, whatever is true, whatever is honorable, whatever is just, whatever is pure, whatever is lovely, whatever is commendable, if there is any excellence, if there is anything worthy of praise, think about these things.*
>
> (PHILIPPIANS 4:8)

Christians' goals for working in society also stand in contrast to others. Their *mission* is not simply to make money, have a satisfying career, do some good in the world, or make things better for others—although all of this can be God-pleasing. Followers of Christ, as masks of God, seek intentionally to be agents of *His* providential care in a world ravaged by sin and the consequences of sin. They acknowledge that God has not abandoned the world to its worst inclinations. Not only has God stepped into the world through the work of Christ, He also continues to curb the constancy of sin through the structures of His created order. He uses ordinary people in families, employment, government, education, the military, the arts, emergencies, healthcare, and so on to mercifully uphold, preserve, and provide for a fallen world. Christians see their mission as *His* mission, to be salt and light as God's representative while giving witness to the hope that is within them (1 Peter 3:15).

Two Regiments—One King

As we have seen, while both believers and nonbelievers function as God's gloves in the world, the Christian's motive, manner, mood, and mission is markedly different. The second important distinction contrasts two different ways of God's operation in the world. Christians acknowledge that God's activity through them occurs in two distinct but overlapping ways. Lutheran theology calls this the doctrine of the two kingdoms, or two realms. Picture a king ruling over a vast domain, simultaneously employing two regiments or assemblies of agents throughout his kingdom. The first regiment—the most important and ultimately most powerful—is called the regiment of the right hand because most kings have dominant right hands (apologies to any left-handed kings out there!). The second regiment—helpful but only of limited strength and influence—includes the agents of his left hand.

The king's right-hand regiment represents the proclamation of the Gospel throughout the world—the spread of the kingdom of God in the hearts of people. God employs ordinary people using ordinary means to bring the message of Christ's death and resurrection to all. Through His Word proclaimed from the pulpit; recorded by the apostles in the Holy Scriptures; announced by His angels; spread by His witnesses; taught through His ministers; spoken, shared, and sung among His people; *and* given through the Sacraments of Baptism and the Lord's Supper, God advances His rule and realm by delivering people from sin, death, and the devil. His right-hand kingdom work comes both as the gift of eternal life through the forgiveness of sins, and also as the gift of becoming new creatures who live new lives motivated by the Gospel. As Martin Luther explained it, "God's kingdom comes when our heavenly Father gives us His Holy Spirit, so that by His grace we believe His holy Word and lead godly lives here in time and there in eternity."[24]

This right-hand kingdom operates through ordinary, humble, sinful servants such as pastors, church workers, and laypeople. It works not by compulsion, but by calling; not by power, but by promise; not by force, but by faith. God the Holy Spirit through the Means of Grace "calls, gathers, enlightens, and sanctifies the whole Christian church on earth, and keeps it with Jesus Christ in the one

24   Small Catechism, Second Petition.

true faith."[25] Through the forgiveness of sins and the assurance of eternal life, God opposes the ravages of sin unleashed by Satan, the corrupting influence of the world, and our rebellious sinful selves. Having been made new creatures through Baptism, Christians also then live out the life of Christ in the various callings God has given them. Through lives of sanctification and godly living, they serve as "salt and light" in a spoiled and darkened world.

> *You are the salt of the earth, but if salt has lost its taste, how shall its saltiness be restored? It is no longer good for anything except to be thrown out and trampled under people's feet. You are the light of the world. A city set on a hill cannot be hidden. Nor do people light a lamp and put it under a basket, but on a stand, and it gives light to all in the house. In the same way, let your light shine before others, so that they may see your good works and give glory to your Father who is in heaven.* (MATTHEW 5:13–16)

On the other hand, the regiment of the king's left also accomplishes important work. God has not abandoned His rebellious creation to the effects of sin. Using ordinary people as His masks, or gloves, God keeps the world from completely tearing itself apart. Thus, police constrain and deter evildoers. Legislatures pass laws for the good of the commonwealth. Teachers inspire and educate children to be productive and creative members of society. Those who work in the fine arts create challenging, beautiful, and meaningful things for the

25   Small Catechism, Third Article.

human spirit. Sanitation workers keep the streets clean. Counselors comfort, advise, and alleviate emotional and psychological pain.

All of this has tremendous value but not ultimate value. If there were no sin, not one of these good and God-pleasing professions would be necessary. Further, their effect is limited to this age. This side of Christ's return, we will never fully remove sin and its costs on our world. It's hard to imagine a time when we won't need police, schools, or hospitals. The word *utopia* literally means "no place." Until Christ returns in glory, our world will constantly be in the throes of sin, death, and the devil. Although from time to time human society can make some external and temporary improvements, these occasional remedies remain ultimately fleeting. Rather like a dying body whose death can be slowed but not prevented and whose pain can be lessened but not removed, the agents of God's left hand do His work of curbing the effects of sin but not its trajectory.

Like God, Christians operate in both kingdoms at the same time—the left and the right. A Christian lawyer serves as God's gloves in the left-hand regiment by being an indispensable part of a society's criminal justice system and by assuring that justice and equity endure. She also receives God's Word at church, bears witness to the resurrection to her neighbors, and teaches her children the faith. A pastor's occupation mainly concerns right-hand regimental duties: expounding the Scriptures, administering the Sacraments, admonishing the erring, comforting the dying, and evangelizing the community. But he also might vote in an election, join the local school board, or serve as a volunteer fireman. Both regiments also contain callings—ordinary ways through which God is active in the world He loves. Farmers, nurses, parents, and welders on the left—church workers, lay-witnesses, and missionaries on the right. All of us, however, function in God's world as His masks—it appears to be us, but God's behind it all.

Life as a Glove

Andrew's wife, Ellen, had an established, well-paying medical career with good benefits. His consulting business had not fully taken off yet, so when their first baby came, they decided Andrew would be a stay-at-home dad for a time. It was an adjustment for all of them—Ellen not wanting to leave them at 7 a.m. to catch the train; Andrew changing diapers, doing the laundry, and trying to build his business while their newborn napped. This was not their Plan A. They had hoped the roles would be reversed, and they prayed this arrangement would be just a season in life for them. They drew great strength from the knowledge that God was also the God of Plan B and tried to remind each other of His work through theirs, His hands through theirs, and His heart through theirs. Andrew changed the diapers—God was behind it. Ellen saw patients at the hospital—God was behind it. Both embraced the fact that each of their present callings contained both blessings and burdens, and that faith in Jesus meant they could approach this season with joyfulness, thankfulness, and contentment.

Bud rises daily with a whistle, usually a tune from one of his favorite hymns. He learned this from his grandfather, who established the family farm three-quarters of a century ago. Grandad always told him to start the day off right, remembering who you are and who this all really belongs to. "It's all the Lord's," he would insist, "the work, the planting, the harvest, the selling, the bounty, and even the profit." The complexities of modern farming—managing workers, expensive equipment, computer systems, and international trade fluctuations—seems a different world compared with his grandfather's. So much has changed, but Bud vows that the most important things never will. He reminds himself, his family, his employees, and even his buyers that God is behind it all. Following his grandfather's example, Bud whispers a short Scripture verse and prayer before his daily work begins or a difficult decision is made: "In His hand is the life of every living thing and the breath of all mankind" (Job 12:10); and "God, be in my hands and in my labors."

No one actually enjoys a middle school band concert. Parents, grandparents, and supportive teachers all smile and say the right things—"Good job! Proud of you! That was really fun!"—but the experience can be unpleasant to the ear and sometimes to the brain. Peter knew all this before deciding to study music education in college, but he chose to go forward with it anyway. The early unpleasant sounds and the maturing musicians are what drew him into this calling in the first place. He does see it as a vocation, in fact, because Peter knows both his gifts and the long-term value of music in society. God has gifted him with exceptional patience, the ability to inspire and motivate young people, and a particular fondness for this age group, no matter how messed up and malevolent they seem. Peter recognizes also that it's not just about the music. Young people need to learn discipline, perseverance, creativity, and cooperation. They need aspirational goals and the gift of perceiving beauty in the world. In a culture so dominated by sports, Peter's "band geeks" have a place and a purpose. The personal formation occurring in these young, sometimes turbulent years will stay with them their whole lives. God is at work through him. The students see Peter's baton, but the music is all God's.

Being born with Down syndrome meant some challenges for Bryan. School was always hard—except the social aspects, of course. Bryan loved people and had a combination of kindness and charisma that drew students to him from all backgrounds and social circles. College wasn't right for him, but after he unveiled his plan to join the village's streets and sanitation crew, his parents couldn't help but feel some disappointment. Bryan knew this would work out, however. He was a hard worker, could handle all the equipment, and would make it a point to get to know as many people in the town as possible.

Flash-forward five years: everybody knows Bryan and loves him. When he picks up your trash in the morning, he'll greet you with a big smile and friendly wave. If you forget to wheel your bin to the curb, he's got you covered. He knows everyone's name and their latest news—who's going on vacation, who has a new dog, when the

Petersen's baby is due. A more cheerful, hardworking, pleasant garbage man won't be found across the globe. What's more, Bryan's faith flows through him. As he greets people in the course of this menial work, he'll always ask if he can pray for them. And he actually does; he adds their name to a simple list next to him in the truck as he tours the neighborhood. He is God's gloves, keeping the community clean and keeping the community connected.

Diego had a gift. He wasn't one to pull straight A's in college or dazzle the professors with academic acumen. Rather, Diego could take fairly difficult concepts, boil them down to their essentials, and explain them to struggling students. He learned this through the back door, in a way. Needing some extra cash his sophomore year, he signed up to tutor freshmen in some required humanities courses—theology, English, and political science. Diego will tell you that he only took the job because it seemed like easy money and fit nicely in his schedule. But by the end of the first semester, he began to experience something else. Those trailblazer students—the first in their families to attend college—felt particular pressure to succeed while receiving little academic support from home. Often both parents worked constantly just to pay the bills (including hefty tuition costs) and didn't have much experience in academia. Diego began to understand his tutoring job as a calling, and in the simple, ordinary activities like helping a struggling student pass freshmen English, he perceived God at work. Diego would teach, explain, encourage, and pray for the students he tutored, but he knew the deeper truth. He was just the mask; God moved behind it all. The experience not only shaped the lives of those he served—a waiting list of freshmen sought his help—it also changed him. Diego decided to switch his major to education and make a career out of it. Sometimes it's not the brightest students who make the greatest teachers. But every great teacher will tell you it's usually the ordinary things that have a life-changing impact.

They couldn't tell you her name, her background, or where she ended up in life, but no member of the family would ever forget her kindness and service to them at their worst moment. Their dad had suffered an aneurysm. It was bad. He wasn't going to make it. The kids flew in from all over the country to be with him, crowding around the hospital bed near their mother for prayers, tears, and even some fun memories to make them laugh out loud through their sadness. Over the course of those three days while their dad's body shut down, one particular nurse aide remained with them. She cared for their beloved father like he was her own, always with tenderness, diligence, and competence. Years later, the family could look back on that difficult time with some spiritual perspective. God had sent that nurse aide to them. She was *His* hands at work, bringing dignity and compassion to a dying father's final hours. They didn't even know her name, but they would never forget her work. She was the gloves of God for them.

A dad raises a family—a farmer, crops. A musician brings a band together—a sanitation worker, the community. A tutor supports a student—a hospital aide, a grieving family. In each of these examples, a seemingly commonplace activity has sacred import because God worked in, through, and behind people to serve His creation. These God-made occupations and opportunities, roles and responsibilities can be effectively accomplished through anyone—believers or not. Christians, however, recognize God's activity through them, rejoice in it, seek to grow in it, and desire God's blessings through it.

The Extraordinary through the Ordinary—Three Biblical Examples

THE BIG FISH—THE BOOK OF JONAH

The best stories have multiple entry points, and this is certainly the case with the world's best-known missionary account, the Book of Jonah. If we're familiar with the narrative, we can easily see ourselves as Jonah: called, but reluctant; knowing God's will, but running clear to the other side of the world to avoid it; crying out to Him from the belly of disobedience, then being spit up right where God needs us;

then, in the end, a bit resentful of God's mercy and kindness toward others. We can all relate to Jonah because we're all called to be missionaries, we're pretty lousy at it, and we can recognize God's grace at work through us despite ourselves.

You might also see yourself in the role of the Ninevites, those called to God through Jonah's preaching. We, too, were once lost in transgression and sin, living in darkness before the light of Christ enlightened us. We, too, have received amazing grace and mercy—undeserved, unsolicited, unbelievable love shown to us in Jesus Christ. We also know that, in a certain sense, the mission work to us is ongoing. We constantly need to be called to repentance and assured of God's continuous mercy to us in Christ.

It sounds risky, but you might even be able to connect to the role of God in the account of Jonah and the big fish. You're not God, of course, but who was the very first missionary? God. Who promised after the fall that the serpent's head would be crushed? Who called His people back through the mouths of the prophets? Who broke into the darkness through the light of Christ in the incarnation? Who called the disciples along the Sea of Galilee? Whose mission took Him to a worse place than Nineveh, to Golgotha, even? Who broke through death to rise on the third day as the greatest missionary ever? God did all this, in the person and work of Jesus Christ. And every great missionary, every Christian called to give witness, can connect to the heart of God that aches in love and mercy for the lost. Ultimately, we are called to be Godlike in our mission work, and although never perfect, we strive to be His instruments in expanding His kingdom.

There is one character in the book, however, with whom you've probably never identified. The whale (big fish, technically). It's not the most flattering part to play, has no lines, and never once does anything dramatic or extraordinary. In fact, the only thing the big fish has to do is . . . well, be a big fish. The fish swims, opens its mouth, eats, digests, poops (presumably), and spits out things that aren't supposed to be in its belly. In a manner of speaking, this pretty much fills out the resume of the fish's vocation—just be what God made it to be. All of this occurred one stormy day many centuries ago as per normal, but God Almighty worked something extraordinary through the mundane work of one of His creatures. God used the ordinary vocation of the big fish to swallow up a prophet, spit him out where he was supposed to be, and bring an entire people back to Himself. We're not told how much the big fish knew about the big picture. Probably not much, being a fish and all. But the most famous missionary account in history would be completely unknown to us had one of God's creatures not fulfilled its creaturely calling.

The Church needs missionaries. All Christians are called to give witness to their faith, and the work of God should remain ever on our hearts. But some of us will need to find contentment and joy in playing the smallest parts on a great stage. Raising children faithfully, working in the world diligently and with integrity, doing menial tasks with meaning, sweating the small stuff—God is at work through all of this, and seldom do we fully understand our role in His greater plan. But take comfort by taking a page from the life of the big fish. First find your calling in the ordinary rather than the dramatic—God will write the rest of the story.

"FOR SUCH A TIME AS THIS"—THE BOOK OF ESTHER

A lustful king, a wicked and scheming official, a beautiful maiden made royal, a righteous leader of an oppressed people. It's all there in the Bible: sex, political intrigue, secret plots, gratuitous violence, inspiring self-sacrifice, and a Hollywood ending as well. The Book of Esther begins five hundred years before Christ with God's Old Testament people scattered throughout the Persian Empire. The self-indulgent Persian king Ahasuerus (sometimes called Xerxes) dismisses his queen, Vashti, mainly because she finally had the audacity to stand up to him. An empire-wide search then gathers the best and the beautiful maidens to be presented before the king for his viewing pleasure and for the selection of a new queen. Meanwhile, the honorable Jewish official Mordecai had adopted his younger cousin, Esther, whose parents had died some years previous. Mordecai loves Esther like his own daughter and, recognizing her great beauty, sees this as an opportunity to give her a better life and improve the status of the Jewish people exiled in Persia. Esther is truly beautiful . . . stunningly beautiful . . . a face that might launch a thousand ships, that kind of beautiful. Always one to know a good thing when he sees it, Ahasuerus takes Esther into his harem and eventually declares her queen.

If that had been the end of the story, the book never would have been written and we never would have heard of the godly Queen Esther. But it isn't the end of the story. The selfish, wicked, and cunning Haman—one of the king's closest advisors—next plots to destroy the Jewish people in Persia. A true egomaniac, Haman manipulates the situation to have all subjects bow and pay homage to him in addition to their obeisance to King Ahasuerus. Mordecai, a faithful Jew who would never bow to a false god, refuses. Enraged, Haman's wrath burns against the entire Jewish people. He prepares legislation and funding for persecution, terror, and the complete destruction of the Jews throughout the Persian Empire.

Haman does not know, however, that the one person closer to the king than he—Queen Esther—is Jewish. Haman also does not count on this young woman possessing greater virtues than beauty. Esther is filled with great courage and integrity in the face of Haman's wickedness. Mordecai gets word to his adopted daughter, Esther, informing her of the impending genocide of their people. Through a clandestine envoy, he pleads with her not to remain silent and to consider that it may have been "for such a time as this" that she rose to such a position (Esther 4:14).

In one of the great biblical moments of courage and boldness for the truth, Esther risks everything—her wealth, her status, and even her life—by pleading the case of her people before the king and thereby exposing the wrathful Haman. She outmaneuvers Haman at court, brings Mordecai into the king's favor, and prevents the horrific destruction of thousands of her people. Haman gets his comeuppance in the end. He's hanged on the seventy-five-foot gallows built to execute Mordecai, and his wealth and position are bestowed on Mordecai and

Esther. To this day, Jewish people throughout the world celebrate Esther's great courage in the festival of Purim.

"For such a time as this." Neither Esther nor Mordecai could possibly have predicted how their choices, their character, and the course of their lives would intersect with the great earthly powers in a time of turmoil. She didn't sign up to be a king's consort in order to unveil a villain and derail a genocide. Rather, in humble service, she used what God had given her—her natural beauty, her trusting relationship with Mordecai, and her deep courage and convictions—in order to do extraordinary things. This is vocation—God's gifts worked through us "for such a time as this."[26]

Although the name of God appears nowhere in the Book of Esther, His presence is found throughout the narrative. He's behind Mordecai's faithfulness and love of his relatives, whose orphaned child he adopts. He's hidden behind Esther's beauty, a natural gift used for a supernatural purpose. He's hidden behind the rise and fall of wicked men and ancient empires. God is behind Mordecai's competence, Esther's courage and character, and even a pagan king's mercurial moods and tumultuous temperament.

Like Esther and Mordecai, none of us can predict the future or control the changes and chances of life. We can, however, stand ready "for such a time as this," when God changes the course of our ordinary lives to intersect with extraordinary things.

INTO THE WEEDS—MOSES AND THE BOOK OF EXODUS

The Book of Exodus tells one of the world's greatest deliverance stories, and it is absolutely true. Here we see God's great power and love working for the rescue of His enslaved people in Egypt, "with a mighty hand and an outstretched arm" (Deuteronomy 26:8). The dramatic and miraculous events have woven their way into the fabric of Western culture: God speaks through a burning bush; twelve

---

26   I am grateful to my colleague Dr. Rachel Eells, who first connected the story of Esther with an understanding of vocation, especially in the use of the biblical phrase "for such a time as this." She presented these ideas to freshmen, Fall Semester, 2019, and at other times during her ministry at Concordia University Chicago.

plagues ravage Egypt; death takes the firstborn on Passover Eve; the Israelites cross the Red Sea; Pharaoh's armies are drowned; and the people journey forty years to the Promised Land. Our world's great books, speeches, music, and movements cannot escape the story of the great escape from Egypt. Jesus Himself discusses His journey to the cross as His exodus (Luke 9:31),[27] and it became the central interpretative principle for the New Testament Church to fully understand Christ's salvific work. The life of the Church, including its ecclesiology, ministry, worship, and Sacraments, is almost indecipherable without reference to Exodus.

If you're not familiar with the book, you should read it (or reread it). Note especially God's dramatic intervention to the life of His people for deliverance, freedom, guidance, and promised rest. One particular moment in the dramatic story is worth a closer look, however, because at a crucial point the purposes of God are fulfilled in the most ordinary, hidden ways. We take up the story in Exodus, chapter 2. Israel has suffered at the hands of the Egyptians for centuries, yet they continue to flourish. Pharaoh's aggression against them reaches its cruel and irrational zenith when he orders the murder of every firstborn Israelite boy. God now begins His intervention, but as we'll see, one of the greatest stories in history begins in the most curious and unassuming manner.

Three women—who hear no voice from God and see no burning bush—take action. Moses' mother builds a basket and hides her beautiful boy among the reeds of the Nile. Moses' sister observes sentry-like from a distance. Pharaoh's daughter rescues the boy, then converses with his watchful sister to arrange for the mother to serve as a nursemaid. Moses is adopted into Pharaoh's household and is raised like a prince, and the story escalates from there to become the great epic known so well.

Three women: no direct command from God, all following the callings of their everyday life, and God remained hidden behind it all. As one preacher put it:

....

27   The Greek word for *departure* is *exodus*.

The actions of hiding, guarding, and rescuing belong to women who are courageous in their defiance, fierce in their devotion, clever and audacious in how they bring the child from the house of slaves to the palace of the Pharaoh. . . .

Instead of God walking through the Garden or proclaiming from the heavens, it is the actions and speech of these women who keep the promise to Abraham moving along . . . these very local and specific human beings who are the hands and feet and eyes of God.[28]

God works through people—simple, sinful, and unknowing though they may be. You might know Moses' sister's name (Miriam). If you're excellent at Bible trivia, you might be able to recall his mother's (Jochebed). Pharaoh's daughter goes unnamed in the biblical account. And yet the story of salvation history, which in fact culminates in the work of Jesus Christ for the salvation of the world, commences through the hands and feet, character and callings of these three ordinary women whom you might not be able to even name. "It is the very hand of God guarding that child for the first three months of his life, protecting the little ark and sister Miriam as she keeps watch, and even in the compassion of Pharaoh's daughter."[29]

It has always been this way with God—doing the extraordinary through the ordinary. And it is a reminder that when we seek to find ourselves in the greater purposes of God, it's best to start small—amid the weeds of the various vocations that God has already placed us.

---

28   Rev. Richard Ramirez, STS, unpublished homily preached in the Chapel of Our Lord, Concordia University Chicago, December 9, 2019. Used with permission.

29   Ramirez homily, 2.

The Four *R*s of an Ordinary Life[30]

God disregards some of the world's greatest, most dramatic achievements while at the same time He gives great and holy significance to the smallest, most mundane, and ordinary tasks. The world and, unfortunately, at times the Church extol the dramatic often at the expense of the ordinary. There can be a less-than-subtle idolatry in this: *my* talents, *my* accomplishments, *my* service, *my* congregation, *my* success. But when we locate our callings first in the commonplace, there's seldom much to boast about. Four important applications stem from understanding that vocation is best discerned in the ordinary rather than the dramatic: *rejoicing* and *relief*; *repentance* and *readiness*.

> *But the LORD said to Samuel, "Do not look on his appearance or on the height of his stature, because I have rejected him. For the LORD sees not as man sees: man looks on the outward appearance, but the LORD looks on the heart."*
>
> (1 SAMUEL 16:7)

A sense of wonder and joy fills us when we recognize God's activity in some of the most common ways. God through *me*! I might not lead a life extolled by the world as notable and accomplished, yet I can rejoice that the God of all living things extends His life-giving and life-preserving providential activity through me. My unpretentious, unremarkable, even unacknowledged tasks, roles, and relationships remain indeed God-callings when done in response to His love, in faith toward Him, and in service to my fellow creatures. No activity

---

30 I am grateful for the discussions from Deaconess Betsy Karkan's Vocation and College Success class, Fall 2019, Concordia University Chicago.

of the Christian done on earth lacks significance and sacred worth when God is active in, through, and behind it. Christians *rejoice* in this knowledge and find peace and contentment in their daily God-breathed activities.

Discovering our callings in the ordinary rather than the dramatic also brings a sense of *relief*. Tremendous personal pressure arises with our heightened expectations of personal achievement. What if I never do anything great? What if I missed my one great calling? What if I was supposed to be doing something earth-shattering, and I'm stuck in the morass of normalcy? Have I failed my parents, my family, or even God? Am I a bad Christian or simply not talented or driven enough to be of any great use for God? Discerning God at work through you, amid the faces, places, and spaces of ordinary life, means nothing further needs to be accomplished but humble faithfulness with the small stuff. God sees, recognizes, and blesses our hands, our feet, our mouths, our minds, our spirits, and our hearts serving in simple ways as His instruments in a fallen and falling world.

> *And whoever gives one of these little ones even a cup of cold water because he is a disciple, truly, I say to you, he will by no means lose his reward.*
>
> (MATTHEW 10:42)

Seeing God at work through the ordinary also convicts us. We are called to *repentance* for seeking first the praise of people or for looking solely to the dramatic all the while neglecting the countless ways God is at work in day-to-day life. We often have a dismissive or disdainful attitude toward the simple and ordinary things, in ourselves and in others. Since they are done in humbleness and lowliness, we might not recognize them as of God, and therefore we might treat them as insignificant or unsacred.

> *But God chose what is foolish in the world to shame the wise; God chose what is weak in the world to shame the strong; God chose what is low and despised in the world, even things that are not, to bring to nothing things that are, so that no human being might boast in the presence of God.* (1 CORINTHIANS 1:27–29)

The Word rightly convicts us when we join the world's celebration of the scintillating rather than rest in the knowledge that God labors through the lowly. When the Holy Spirit shows us our sinfulness, He also then reveals the precious news that Christ Jesus has indeed dealt with all our sin in the fullest way possible. He took on our ordinary flesh and blood, lived our earthly life, and carried a hard and heavy cross all the way to death and through death, for us. Christ was made low for us, that we might be exalted with Him in resurrection life. Repenting of our sins, we also then take comfort in the knowledge of the Gospel—redemption in His name.

> *My soul magnifies the Lord, and my spirit rejoices in God my Savior, for He has looked on the humble estate of His servant. For behold, from now on all generations will call me blessed; for He who is mighty has done great things for me, and holy is His name. And His mercy is for those who fear Him from generation to generation. He has shown strength with His arm; He has scattered the proud in the thoughts of their hearts; He has brought down the mighty from their thrones and exalted those of humble estate; He has filled the hungry with good things, and the rich He has sent away empty. He has helped His servant Israel, in remembrance of His mercy, as He spoke to our fathers, to Abraham and to his offspring forever.* (LUKE 1:46–55)

Finally, certain that God works through them in ordinary callings, baptized believers in Jesus stand at the *ready* for whatever might unfold for them. This includes first and foremost a life of sanctification. In the smallest and most commonplace ways, the Spirit does new things in the new creatures remade through the Gospel. This means that like Bryan (see above), we strive for virtuous lives in the stations into which God has placed us. Employees work hard and play fair in industry and business. Supervisors manage fairly and equitably, but also firmly when necessary. Children avoid laziness, disobedience, and disrespectfulness, seeking to honor God in their relationships at home, at school, and at play. Mothers and fathers parent as God's instruments, not disciplining out of self-indulgence or uncontrolled anger, but always with the good of the child above their personal needs or emotions. Healthcare workers and others in the helping professions serve patients and clients with the care and conscientiousness they would offer their own loved ones. Those given civic authority or political power rule not for themselves or for their own tribal agenda, but equitably, reasonably, dispassionately, and sacrificially, placing the needs of the community above oneself. When Christians recognize that they are but the masks of God in the structures of His creation, they seek the highest and most helpful virtues for the world they serve.

> *I appeal to you therefore, brothers, by the mercies of God, to present your bodies as a living sacrifice, holy and acceptable to God, which is your spiritual worship. Do not be conformed to this world, but be transformed by the renewal of your mind, that by testing you may discern what is the will of God, what is good and acceptable and perfect.* (ROMANS 12:1–2)

Further, living out their baptismal callings amid a broken world, Christians stand at the ready for when God calls them "for such a time as this." Like Esther, they may have ascended to a place of influence or power in a company or community, the church or the state. They may be asked to make difficult choices and bold confessions, or live the truth regardless of the consequences. Like the women of Exodus 2,

Christians may one day lift up their eyes of faith and marvel at the unexpected story being written around them amid the mundane tasks God gave them to fulfill. With the big fish in the Book of Jonah, they may live their creaturely lives just being who God made them to be. Faithfully fulfilling their earthly callings, they may never fully know or understand the eternal impact of their service. And like the list of all-star saints hung in sacred stadiums, their callings begun in the ordinary may even be moved by God to become world-altering or life-changing for thousands. But in any case and in each case, Christians "at the ready" remain humble in their service, glorify God in their accomplishments, and serve or suffer cheerfully for the sake of Christ, who works in, through, and behind them.

For Discussion

1. Write a thank-you note to a Christian "all-star" who has significantly impacted your faith. This person could be biblical, historic, or personal.

2. What do you find inspiring about Rosa Young's speech (page 58)?

3. What is the "beginning of any great task and a virtue of any great person" (page 61)?

4. What was helpful about Matt's advice to Abigail as she considered serving in the church (page 63)?

5. Can you share a time in your life when you felt you needed a "letter from God" like Jayla's (pages 65–66)? Do you know someone who might need such a word of encouragement?

6. Discuss the difficulty of seeing your everyday, ordinary callings as "golden and noble works" (page 66).

7. Read again Martin Luther's comments extolling the mundane callings of marriage and family (page 67). Why might his words seem so radical at the time?

8. Explain what it means that we serve as "masks of God" or "gloves of God" (pages 69–70). How is a Christian's service different from a nonbeliever's (pages 70–73)?

9. What is important to note about the big fish's role in the account of Jonah (pages 81–82)?

10. Have you ever felt that you were placed somewhere "for such as time as this" (pages 82–84)? What's the best way to prepare yourself for how God might use you in the future?

11. What's important and surprising about the roles of the three women in the great Exodus epic (page 85)?

12. What are the "four Rs of an ordinary life," and why are they important to remember (pages 87–92)?

CHAPTER 4

GOD LOVES DIRT

*Our calling in life is better understood as
this-worldly rather than otherworldly.*

God loves dirt. God made dirt. After creating all other living things through the power of His Word, God knelt down into the dust, forming humanity with His own hands. God touched the good earth, placed His mouth on it, and breathed into it the breath of His life. The very name for the first man, Adam, comes from the Hebrew word for earth (*adamah*). The rest of creation God was content to speak into existence: the galaxies and stars, the beasts of the fields and birds of the air; the invisible structures of time, space, and gravity. But with human beings, God got His hands dirty.

> *Then the LORD God formed the man of dust from the ground and breathed into his nostrils the breath of life, and the man became a living creature.* (GENESIS 2:7)

God made the creation *real*—physical, corporeal, flesh, blood, and bones—and God said that it was good. Nothing incomplete or corrupt infected the creation. It was not half-finished, half-baked, or a mistaken malformation deriving from a higher-level spiritual war, marriage, or miscarriage, as pagan creation myths have it. In an act of freedom and love, God brought all of creation into existence and never needed it to be anything but what He made it to be. From the crown of creation (human beings), to the littlest creepy worm in the ground, God endowed His world with inherent worth. Matter mattered to God.

> *Then God said, "Let Us make man in Our image, after Our likeness. And let them have dominion over the fish of the sea and over the birds of the heavens and over the livestock and over all the earth and over every creeping thing that creeps on the earth." So God created man in His own image, in the image of God He created him; male and female He created them.* (GENESIS 1:26–27)

This is important to note because, in fact, it sails against the prevailing winds of much of our society and even against certain movements within Christianity, ancient and modern. To be sure, our created world now is broken, sinful, and in rebellion against God as we live outside of the garden. This is probably where some of the confusion lies. We misdiagnose the symptoms as the disease. The problem is not the existence of the created world itself, as if some design flaw or structural defect inevitably led to an obvious major malfunction. No. God made it good, and it would have remained good had not human pride and rebellion shunned its creaturely goodness and strove rather to "be like God" (Genesis 3:5). Before sin, everything from the sand to the stars had the declaration of "good" from the mouth of the Almighty Himself. God loves dirt.

Though this world is obscured by the reality of sin, we can still discern some of the beauty and goodness of God's handiwork. A busy pastor will tell you how much he enjoys gardening on his day off. There's unquestionably something therapeutic about getting your hands dirty and growing something green. There's a reason children love to build sandcastles or snow forts outside in the fresh air and sunshine. These timeless pastimes can even out-compete the allure of endless screen time for our kids. Have you ever wondered why, after spending centuries perfecting the comforts of modern housing, camping remains one of the most popular outdoor activities? More than 60 percent of US households (75 million people) describe themselves as active campers, and the number is expected to grow. It's never been more popular with young people,[31] and the value for the educational development of children is unquestioned in the academic literature. Even the color green—the most abundant pigment on our landmasses, a color that remains mostly *outside*—demonstrably offers calming effects on the human spirit.[32]

Our physical, social, and emotional selves are inseparable. It's one thing to simply eat alone for nourishment; it's another to invite someone over for a meal; and still another thing to actually prepare and cook a meal with friends. Any successful treatment for depression or anxiety will include healthy eating and regular exercise as a component for change. Athletes work out *together* for accountability but also for community. Spouses enjoy home repairs not simply because it's cheaper than hiring a contractor but because shared work brings them together. Anyone in ministry will attest to the value of healthy physical touch. A deaconess holds the hand of a dying congregant; a preschool teacher hugs her students; a youth worker high-fives a high school graduate; a pastor makes the sign of the cross over a baby's head and heart.

The overall case is compelling: the mundane matters. Earthy and earthly existence, though marred by sin, still carries an imprint

31   "Camping Is Up in the U.S., Trend Expected to Continue as Millennials Seek the Positive Health Impacts of Time Spent Outdoors," BusinessWire, accessed January 10, 2020, https://www.businesswire.com/news/home/20170315005391/en/Camping-U.S.-Trend-Expected-Continue-Millennials-Seek.

32   Morton Walker, *The Power of Color* (New York: Avery, 1990). I am grateful to Brinn Miller, CUC `23, for this reference.

from the Creator, who made it good and, in the incarnation of Jesus Christ, physically came to redeem it to Himself. In the beauty of their existence before sin, human beings ate, worked, and enjoyed sex in the procreation of children (see Genesis 2 and 3). God gave them fruit to enjoy, Adam named the animals and tended the garden, and the male and female human creatures joined together in sexual union under the boundaries and blessings of God. The fact that all this occurred before there was sin and rebellion demonstrates that God has given a sacred significance to every aspect of our physical existence. At no point has He ever asked us to be anything but a fully physical, created being. Nothing "higher" needs to be achieved or accomplished; nothing physical needs to be escaped from or transcended. We were created good—body, mind, and spirit—right from the beginning when God grabbed the dirt and breathed life into us.

The "Climb" into Sin

It's common to talk about humanity's original rebellion against God as "the fall." Although there's great value in this, another and perhaps more helpful way of talking about it is as "the climb." God's human creatures, together with His good creation in all its physical wonder, exist in peace and contentment being what God made them to be. The serpent tempts them not so much to become lower but to reach higher. "You will be like God" (Genesis 3:5), hisses the evil one. Doubting God's Word and disparaging their simple creatureliness, Eve and then Adam climb over each other in order to reach their way up to God. The whole scope of sin in the world is arguably best described as a wicked, discontented ascent away from the satisfaction of blessed earthly existence. Satan and his angels rise up against God. Adam and Eve irrationally desire more than all God has given. The tower of Babel soars up toward heaven. James and John, the sons of thunder, desire the higher places in the kingdom. Pride, greed, covetousness, envy, and lust all flow from the one common sin of seeking at the expense or exploitation of others to rise above one's creaturely contentment.

> The root of all sin is pride, *superbia*. I want to be
> for myself; I have a right to be myself, a right to
> my hatred and my desires, my life and my death.
> The spirit and flesh of human beings are inflamed
> by pride, for it is precisely in their wickedness that
> human beings want to be like God.[33]

The climb into sin is universal, destructive, irrational, and pervasive. All human beings participate in it regardless of ethnicity, cultural background, age, gender, or economic status. It tears down all aspects of society, leading to war, injustice, and the exploitation of others. It doesn't make sense either. Adam and Eve had all they needed in the garden—an abundance of tasty fruit, sacred work, and fellowship with each other and their Creator. And yet they wanted the one thing God had said no to. This condition of the climb is not a surface-level problem, one that can simply be legislated or educated away. Rather, it saturates the soul of every human being in history, and its consequences are deadly and inescapable. One could say, then, that sin is not so much a falling back into physicality or becoming too earthy; rather, it is a twisting or corrupting of the God-given physical world for selfish, self-serving ends. The solution was not an escape *from* the created order but a redemption and renewal of it.

Jesus Redeems the Dirt

The good news of the Gospel is not just that God saved us. It crucially includes precisely *what* about us He has saved. God redeemed the fullness of all that it means to be a human creature, including our earthly, physical essence. God in Christ became a real, physical

---

33   Bonhoeffer, *Life Together*, 111.

human being. He redeemed us not by taking us out of this world or giving us release from the prison of earthy, fleshly existence. Rather, God stepped into humanity, into creation, in the person and work of Jesus Christ, who was fully human as well as fully God. Christ was conceived by the Holy Spirit in the womb of a human mother. Though also divine, His human nature developed as any human embryo does, carefully formed and intimately woven.

> *For You formed my inward parts; You knitted me together in my mother's womb. I praise You, for I am fearfully and wonderfully made. Wonderful are Your works; my soul knows it very well. My frame was not hidden from You, when I was being made in secret, intricately woven in the depths of the earth. Your eyes saw my unformed substance; in Your book were written, every one of them, the days that were formed for me, when as yet there was none of them.* (PSALM 139:13–16)

As a human child, Jesus matured, learned, and grew. As a young man, He went through puberty. He studied a trade to work with His hands as a carpenter. He developed friendships and familial ties in the culture and community of His homeland. Anything a human being can do, think, be, or become without sin, Jesus did. This includes without reservation a physical life of growing, eating, sleeping, running, thinking, feeling, and so on. This truth is not just theologically important, it is personally important. Consider an aspect of your creaturely existence that has been tainted with sin (there's plenty to choose from, I am sure). In order for Christ to fulfill the Law, He would need also to complete the fullness of your human life in every aspect in which you have failed. If He had not become fully human in its manifold aspects, something of sin would remain for you. But thanks be to God that, indeed, Christ Jesus fully embraced human life in the incarnation as the new Adam for all, and that by being baptized into Him, we have new life in Him.

> *Since then we have a great high priest who has passed through the heavens, Jesus, the Son of God, let us hold fast our confession. For we do not have a high priest who is unable to sympathize with our weaknesses, but one who in every respect has been tempted as we are, yet without sin. Let us then with confidence draw near to the throne of grace, that we may receive mercy and find grace to help in time of need.* (HEBREWS 4:14–16)

In His earthly and earthy ministry, Jesus "got down and dirty," so to speak, in restoring the lost creation. He used His human mind in theological conversations with rabbinic experts (Luke 2:41–47). Bitter tears flowed down His cheeks at the death of a dear friend (John 11:35, 38). His pure hands touched the diseased skin of a leper (Mark 1:40–43). He used spittle and dirt to restore blind eyes (John 9:6–7). The human hand of Jesus reached into rough water to rescue a drowning Peter (Matthew 14:28–31) and touched death, bringing life to a dead girl (Mark 5:41–42). In the actions, activities, and attitudes of His ministry among us, Jesus both embraced and restored all that was wrong with the creation. In love, He did not abandon His creation to its destructive rebellion, but neither did He remove it from its earthy origins. Jesus descended into the dirt, declaring it good again through His word and work.

> *Have this mind among yourselves, which is yours in Christ Jesus, who, though He was in the form of God, did not count equality with God a thing to be grasped, but emptied Himself, by taking the form of a servant, being born in the likeness of men. And being found in human form, He humbled Himself by becoming obedient to the point of death, even death on a cross. Therefore God has highly exalted Him and bestowed on Him the name that is above every name, so that at the name of Jesus every knee should bow, in heaven and on earth and under the earth, and every tongue confess that Jesus Christ is Lord, to the glory of God the Father.* (PHILIPPIANS 2:5–11)

In the crucifixion, Christ's embrace of the rebellious creation reached its inevitable, horrifying consequences. In direct contrast to Adam and Eve's climb into sin, where they disdain creaturely contentment and seek the place of God, Christ Jesus sets aside His divinity and seeks the lowest place of humanity. Naked, shame-filled, and sin-infested, He dies our death on an instrument of human torture. This was a real death, with real thorns in His head, rips on His back, and nails through His flesh and bones. No phantom voice cried out to His heavenly Father. No idealized mythic symbol of death and new life unfolded that Friday. No zealous followers stormed the hill to rescue or replace their teacher at His worst hour. This was not a "spiritual" death that only seemed real on the outside. A man suffered, a mother cried, and a heart stopped. All the realities of death, with all that means for every human being who has ever lived and died, Christ Jesus experienced on that day when life and death contended.

> It was a strange and dreadful strife
> When life and death contended;
> The victory remained with life,
> The reign of death was ended.
> Holy Scripture plainly saith
> That death is swallowed up by death,
> Its sting is lost forever. Alleluia!
>
> *LSB 458:4*

The reality of Jesus' death is important not just because it demonstrates Christ's great love for us—although this is most certainly true. It is important because it also acknowledges the reality of human physical death and pain as the consequences of sin. If Christ's death had not been painfully real, our own painfully real deaths could have no other end and no other meaning. But through His sacrificial death on the cross, Christ Jesus atones fully for the sins of the whole world by descending fully into the depths of our rebellious creation.

Christ's sacrificial death was fully physical, and equally physical was His victory over death in the resurrection. This also was no phantom, spiritual, or symbolic new life. As alive as a human being can be, so alive was the risen Christ. This is why the post-resurrection appearances recorded in the Gospels contain such corporeal content. Jesus walked with disciples on the road to Emmaus (Luke 24:13–35). He shared a meal with them (Luke 24:36–43). He cooked breakfast with them, consuming broiled fish on the beach (John 21:9–13). He didn't just show them His hands and feet but directed the doubters to touch and feel for themselves (Luke 24:39; John 20:27). And when they would reflect back on their time with Jesus after His ascension, the disciples joyfully gave witness to the physical reality of all that had happened: eternity stepped into time, manna became man, love became alive in Jesus Christ.

> *That which was from the beginning, which we have heard, which we have seen with our eyes, which we looked upon and have touched with our hands, concerning the word of life—the life was made manifest, and we have seen it, and testify to it and proclaim to you the eternal life, which was with the Father and was made manifest to us—that which we have seen and heard we proclaim also to you, so that you too may have fellowship with us; and indeed our fellowship is with the Father and with His Son Jesus Christ. And we are writing these things so that our joy may be complete.*
>
> (1 JOHN 1:1–4)

The reality of the restoration of creation through Christ's bodily resurrection means also the physical new creation one day for all who believe and are baptized into the work of Christ. Contrary to popular misconceptions even among Christians, our final salvation will not be as disembodied spirits, floating around in an ethereal eternal existence somewhere. After death, our souls will rest with Christ in peace and bliss. But at the final resurrection when Christ returns, our souls and bodies will be reunited and physical existence will be restored. We will live as Adam and Eve did, with real, glorified bodies in a new heaven and a new earth. There is much we do not know and cannot fully comprehend about our eternal life with God. But what remains certain is that it will be as real as a meal shared, a loving hug, and tears of joyful reunion. Jesus Christ will redeem, resurrect, and renew the dirt.

Until that time after time, Christians have their sinful bodies renewed in the life of Christ's sanctified body, the "one holy Christian and apostolic Church," as we say in the Nicene Creed. Real words from the Holy Scriptures both kill and bring to life on our earthly pilgrimage. Regular, plain water combines with God's Word to drown the old Adam and graft us into the new Adam, Jesus Christ. The common elements of bread and wine are Christ's true body and blood for the real forgiveness, life, and salvation of human beings living in a sin-filled world. In all of this and in the very act of His salvation for us in Jesus Christ, God demonstrates the goodness of created, earthly, and earthy things. God loves dirt, and He redeemed it through the work of His Son.

The Quest for the Super-Spiritual: Being "like God"

Christianity has often struggled with a tendency to hate the body, despise the mundane, and seek the otherworldly by escaping from the responsibilities of this world. In the world of the Early Church, extremist forms of asceticism dominated non-Christian, heretical, and Christian forms of monasticism. These movements, of course, had many important points of contrast. Pagan groups completely denied a Creator God and the work of Christ. Heretical groups, as we shall see, claimed the name "Christian" but confused or distorted the truth of Christ to an unrecognizable form. Fringe Christian groups, though retaining the essentials of biblical teaching, veered dangerously adrift and off course. One tendency, however, united them: the assumption that anything of the physical world is inherently bad by the mere fact of its created existence. The world, its activities, and its patterns of life remained a lesser state from which enlightened or empowered human beings could achieve release. This is why vegetarianism and virginity were greatly extolled in all these ascetic movements. The corporeal was corrupt; the physical more fallible than the spiritual. The mundane matters of the world—farming, family, business, governing, labor—captured the essential human soul, keeping it from its place with the divine.

One such movement, called Gnosticism, dangerously threatened the Christian faith. Deriving from the Greek word for knowledge (*gnōsis*), Gnosticism is best understood not as a uniform religion with a canon of agreed upon sacred texts, organized structures, and codified doctrines but rather as a complex movement of religious thought, pervading the Roman intellectual world in the second and third centuries AD. Gnostics dealt with the problem of evil by postulating that the world was created by an evil, lesser god—a demiurge—whose work opposed the true and transcendent God. Release from the prison house of created matter could be achieved only through a secret knowledge (*gnōsis*) sent down from God through a revealer, whose teaching on reality and destiny released the true spiritual nature of those imprisoned by the flesh. Heretical Christian forms of Gnosticism cast Christ in the part of truth revealer and were rigorously opposed by Christian theologians such as Irenaeus, Hippolytus, and Tertullian. Some Gnostics, once "awakened," ironically overindulged in carnal desires (thinking that if the physical didn't ultimately matter, then it couldn't really corrupt them). Most, however, tried to flee from the influences of the corrupted matter and were admired for their radical asceticism. Freeing oneself from the shackles of sinful matter revealed a true, inner, spiritual self.

One of the Gnostic corruptions of Christian doctrine is a Christological heresy called Docetism (literally "seems" in Greek). Because anything of physical existence was by definition corrupt, made by an evil god in opposition to the Good and Transcendent, Christ's incarnation into human flesh and blood as well as His bodily death became problematic. Wishing to retain the figure of Christ as wise secret-revealer, some Gnostics claimed that He only appeared (seemed) human but in reality remained always wholly other than the created world. In direct opposition to Docetism, Christianity asserted the actual physical conception, birth, life, and death of Jesus Christ, both truly God and truly man.

A later but related heresy called Manichaeism renewed this assault on the essential good of God's creation and thus upon the human nature of Christ. The Manichees followed the teaching of Mani (AD 216–77), a Persian aristocrat who claimed his direct visions from God validated his role as "the last of the prophets of God, bearing the whole and final truth, of which previous religions had been but partial manifestations."[34] Although Mani claimed to be an apostle of Jesus Christ, his teachings are at best a deformed version of the true faith. Like previous forms of Gnosticism, the Manichees posited two opposing gods—one evil principle of the lower forms of dark particles and one good, from whom stemmed the higher particles of light. The created universe was formed in a cosmic conflict between these two principles, the light being captured and imprisoned by the dark. Mani's message of "salvation" called his followers to free themselves from their "fleshly bonds, and ascend to the Paradise of Light."[35] Through an inner illumination of Christ, the Manichean elect strove to abstain from all earthly activities—eating meat, having sex, farming, war, commerce—and in so doing not only free themselves but also facilitate the process of releasing the light particles from the dark for the liberation of the universe.

---

34   Gerald Bonner, *St. Augustine of Hippo: Life and Controversies*, 3rd ed. (Norwich: Canterbury Press, 2002), 159.

35   Bonner, *St. Augustine*, 167.

The Manichean faith . . . must be reckoned among the strangest and most bizarre of the many strange and bizarre fantasies which the human mind has conceived.[36]

Although myths like these appear comically bizarre to us, at least one core principle of their teachings arises continually to challenge Christianity: your true inner self is not comprised of physical, earthly matter but in fact can only be truly discovered in liberation from the world. The "real you" isn't real, so to speak. Escaping from the lower, darker, evil "stuff" of earthly existence brings illumination and salvation. God doesn't love dirt. Creation was a mistake. Goodness can be found only in escape. Matter not only doesn't matter, it's the source of evil. False notions like these, stemming from the original sin of the garden, cause discontentment with our creatureliness, tempting us to ascend to "be like God."

A variation on the same theme, let's call it "spiritual escapism," arose also in the late medieval religious orders. The traditional threefold vows of celibacy, poverty, and obedience originally stemmed from a need for reform in the twelfth and thirteenth centuries, serving to protect the Church from political and feudal influence. Celibate clergy could not engage in nepotism—simply passing on their positions to their heirs. Members of a religious order owned no personal property, so they could not buy and sell their offices. They could fully engage in spiritual matters, undistracted by the necessities of labor and income. Their allegiance was exclusively to their monastic superiors, shielding them from any outside political influence. One can see, however, how easily the desire to protect the Church from worldly

---

36   Bonner, *St. Augustine*, 157.

corruption could devolve into a dismissive attitude toward the gifts of God's good creation.

Martin Luther's reforms included a bitter attack on the theology and practices of the sixteenth-century religious orders. He found two themes particularly diabolical. First, those in the religious life regarded withdrawal from the world as not just helpful but even necessary. They thought it impossible to fully serve God without withdrawing to a higher spirituality, a nobler and closer-to-God life away from earthly concerns. Second, the Medieval Church regarded good works such as celibacy, poverty, fasting, pilgrimages, and so on as "acts of supererogation"—super-works beyond those required in the Ten Commandments. And because they considered them above and beyond, these higher spiritual activities and disciplines were thought to overflow into the lives of regular people. They could be applied to those necessarily mired in the world, such as farmers, soldiers, and craftsmen. A "treasury of merit" stored the benefits of these super-works, which could be distributed to repentant sinners through the Catholic Church's system of indulgences.

Luther vehemently objected to this system's corruption of the Gospel. It did not ground our standing before God solely in the grace received through faith in Christ's work. But Luther also detected in the late medieval religious life the recurring theme of "spiritual escapism" and regarded it as a denial of God's redemption of His beloved creation. Instead, Luther taught Christians to discover their callings in the God-pleasing activities of God's redeemed world. *Callings should be understood as this-worldly rather than the otherworldly* because it is precisely this world that needs God. Spiritual escapism helped no one but the devil, he argued, and in fact, more often than not, it led to arrogance, elitism, and false doctrine. Historian Marc Kolden expressed Luther's insights this way:

> Just as God's redemptive act in becoming incarnate affirms that salvation is not an escape from creation but a restoration and fulfillment of it, so also the Christian life will not be an escape from creaturely

life but a calling to it. The call to follow Christ leads not to any religious vocation removed from daily life, but instead it transforms the attitude and understanding one has of the situation in which one already is.[37]

This incarnational understanding of vocation is important because new forms of spiritual escapism will always arise, tempting us *away from* rather than *into* the matter and matters of creaturely life. We are certainly called to "be like God" in love, service, and holy living in this world. We are not called to "be like God" by being wholly other, released from this world. We are and must always remain creatures—redeemed, though sinful—finding callings, ministry, and mission in the world He still loves and will ultimately restore in wholeness and holiness.

The real work of God is in the dirt. In the mess. In the world of service for the neighbor. Luther criticized the monastic orders because they weren't doing anything particularly useful. In fact, they were doing something harmful—teaching falsely about purgatory and good works. But also, their sacred escapism had caused a misdefining of *vocatio*, applying it only to those who could achieve otherworldly status. Luther recovered the true sense of *vocatio*, applying it not just to the spiritual elite but to all. This meant that the most mundane tasks, the most common, worldly occupations could have sacred, holy, spiritual significance. God loves dirt.

---

37   Marc Kolden, "Luther on Vocation," *Word & World* 3/4 (1983): 387.

In the medieval church, having a vocation or having "a calling" referred exclusively to full-time church work. If a person felt a calling, this was a sign that he or she might "have a vocation," which meant becoming a priest, a monk, or a nun. The ordinary occupations of life—being a peasant farmer or kitchen maid, making tools or clothing, being a soldier or even king—were acknowledged as necessary but *worldly*. Such people could be saved, but they were mired in the world. To serve God fully, to live a life that is truly *spiritual*, required a full-time commitment. The "counsels of perfection" could be fulfilled only in the Holy Orders of the church, in which a man or woman could devote every day to prayer, contemplation, worship, and the service of God.[38]

GENE EDWARD VEITH JR.

The Allure of the Otherworldly

Rodney had grown weary of it all: late-night shifts at the convenience store, getting up early to feed his two-year-old son, tidying up the house, doing laundry, working two jobs. No one doubts the difficulties of the life of a single dad, and certainly his parents' support for him, letting him stay with them for a while, didn't go unappreciated.

38   Gene Edward Veith Jr., *God at Work* (Wheaton, IL: Crossway Books, 2002), 17–18, emphasis added. Used by permission of Crossway, a publishing ministry of Good News Publishers, Wheaton, IL 60187, www.crossway.org.

But Rodney was *done*. The mundane matters of work and home seemed so unspiritual and unimportant. In fact, Rodney began to think that the daily drudgery was the problem. He didn't like himself anymore, as his tired, cranky, resentful self arose more often than the cheerful guy everyone loved to be around.

Seeking an escape from the hard work of daily life, Rodney got more involved with a "holiness" church down the street. His parents and friends thought initially that this would be a good thing for him.

Before long, however, they got a better sense of what was really going on. More prayer meetings, the desire for deeper spiritual experiences, yet another retreat away from work and family all added up to Rodney avoiding the hard work of real life and real responsibilities, to the point where his absence was noticeably affecting his young son. Rodney had plenty of excuses. Like an all-star shortstop fielding grounders, he effortlessly dispatched with his family's legitimate concerns: "But I need to realize my true, inward spiritual self." "This world is only holding back my progression toward God." "The Bible calls me to seek the higher things." "The things of this world are all temporary and fleeting anyway." Half-truths lined his excuses, just like they did the serpent's in the garden. It took a hard word of *full* truth from Rodney's mom to bring him back to earth. "We need you down here, Son" she admonished him. "These *are* the higher things of God. Quit using your quest to climb up to heaven to avoid what's difficult here on earth."

Rodney's story is Episode 1 in a miniseries we might call "Sacred Escapism." Sometimes we use the excuse of the super-spiritual to avoid the hard work of real life. This world is messy. Dealing with sin in ourselves and in one another is never easy because it requires honesty, repentance, forgiveness, and new life by the Spirit. It's easier to try to escape from the world—and we can even fool ourselves into thinking this is a higher, more spiritual endeavor. The truth is, life in the body is hard. That's why the forgiveness of Christ is for real people with real sin. Rodney's story warns us against using the pretense of an otherworldly quest because we don't want to deal with the this-worldly mess.

• •

> **Regardless of the lives and examples of all saints, each man ought to learn patiently what God commands him, and to discharge faithfully his own vocation. . . . See, you find many people who do all sorts of things, but not what they have been commanded to do. Someone hears that some saints went on a pilgrimage and were praised for that. Then this fool goes ahead, leaves behind the wife and child for whom God has made him responsible, runs to St. James, or here or there, and does not realize that his vocation and command are completely different from that given to the saint he is following.**[39]

• •

Episode 2 stars a woman in her twenties named Alyssa. She's *always* at church because, well, she works there. She does family ministry at a large congregation in a beautiful suburb near Denver. Alyssa's call into full-time ministry arose out of a difficult past and a life of ungodly living. Although she's open about her story before she came to faith, there's still a tinge of shame when she explains the dark places she roamed in body, mind, and spirit. No doubt her decision to serve the church professionally stemmed from a sincere faith and the desire to tell others about God's grace in Jesus Christ. But in her honest moments, she could admit that part of her still was trying to work off her sins. By escaping the life of the world to the

---

39   Martin Luther, translated by Gustaf Wingren, *Luther on Vocation* (Evansville, IN: Ballast Press, 2004), 203. Used by permission of Wipf and Stock Publishers. www.wipfandstock.com. Cf. Lenker (ed.) *Sermons of Martin Luther*, vol. 1, 241.

life of the church, Alyssa had run as far away from the real world as possible—part in shame, part in fear that she would fall back into old habits, and part in self-righteousness. Alyssa confesses that at times she possessed a rather disparaging attitude toward other vocations. She was doing the *real* work of God, you know. The mothers and maids, truckers and teachers in her congregation were involved in mundane matters. She was doing the spiritual work, and thank goodness she was, otherwise it would never get done!

Alyssa's episode has a happy ending because the moms group she started at church called her out on it. It was probably the most difficult conversation she'd had since becoming a Christian, but she knew they were right. Sometimes our strivings to "be like God" can become self-made super-works that we subconsciously employ to pay off our sins. The trap is that there's just as much sin in the spiritual stuff as the earthly stuff—ask anyone who's ever worked or volunteered in the church. Often this leads to even greater disillusionment because we think that a church, Christian community, or Christian institution is supposed to be different. It's supposed to be about higher things. And when we discover that spiritual escapism doesn't lead to less sin, we're especially disappointed. Alyssa figured this out because the people she served ultimately served her by gently but firmly confronting her. She now looks at her calling differently. It's not higher or more spiritual than that of the other members of her congregation simply because they're involved in earthly activities. Rather, their callings are as equally spiritual as hers because they are led by the Spirit in response to the Gospel. Alyssa received a fresh sense of joy and contentment in her calling to church work as well. As she tells it, her work in family ministry matches well with her gifts and passions. It's a choice she's made to serve this way, free from guilt or self-righteousness and truly as a "response-ability"—using her abilities in response to what Christ has done for her. It's a special calling, she'll tell you, but not a higher or more heavenly calling than the callings of the people she serves.

> It follows from this argument that there is no true, basic difference between laymen and priests, princes and bishops, between religious and secular, except for the sake of office and work, but not for the sake of status. They are all of the spiritual estate, all are truly priests, bishops, and popes. But they do not all have the same work to do. MARTIN LUTHER, LW 44:129

Episode 3 is the hardest of all to watch because it deals with a heart-wrenching tragedy. James will always remember that snowy morning when the sheriff and pastor showed up at his office: a tragic highway accident, an overturned semi-truck and trailer, and three precious faces he'll never see alive again. His wife and two young children were killed that morning in one of the most horrific accidents that county had seen in decades. You never get over something like that, but James had a strong extended family and a church community that embraced him and walked with him every step of the way.

> *I have said these things to you, that in Me you may have peace. In the world you will have tribulation. But take heart; I have overcome the world.* (JOHN 16:33)

Fast-forward five painful years. Both the large and small questions still haunted him: "Couldn't God have intervened? Why them on that particular morning? What did they feel or think right as it happened?

What if I had decided to drive them to school that morning because of the weather?" Some of his questions were head-based—"It's hard to wrap your head around an almighty God who loves us but allows this to happen." Some of them were heart-based—"I hope they didn't suffer." Mostly, he just missed them. He longed to sit next to his beloved wife on early winter mornings, sipping coffee and chatting; he wished just once more to tuck his kids into bed after reading a favorite bedtime story.

James's story takes another tragic turn because his understandable questions arising from unspeakable grief caused him to withdraw more and more from this world and from those who loved him. His drinking got out of hand. He lost his job. He stopped going to church because the community, hymns, songs, and readings pained him as reminders of what he lost. He even started experimenting with new-age religion, crystals, and meditation—all in an attempt to escape from this world, which had betrayed him so cruelly and hurt him so deeply. Like some of the religious movements of ages past that promised a higher spiritual enlightenment away from the sufferings of this world, James was drawn to a release from pain by a release to a higher plane. The truth is, however, that he won't be able to get around his grief. He can only pass through it. There's no escaping the hard reality of sin and death for any of us.

The ending of Episode 3 hasn't been written yet. James is still searching and waiting. There will be no easy answers or pat Bible passages to fix it for him. He won't open a sympathy card from a well-meaning friend and suddenly find peace. But what someone will need to let him know is that his attempts to escape from his pain by escaping from this world will prove fruitless. His calling remains in this world, although his hope is in the life of the world to come, where he will hold his precious ones again. Christ Jesus stepped into our pain-filled world, enfleshing and enmeshing Himself fully in sin, suffering, and death. When He bore the cross for the sins of the world, He promised that we would never bear our crosses alone. And in His bodily resurrection on the third day, He proclaimed that life and love will have the last word on us. What Jesus didn't do was promise an easy release from this world or assure us that no suffering will afflict us. His calling is always back into the world, as difficult as this might be. His promise is that He will walk with us in those callings, giving us grace and strength for whatever lies ahead.

> *For I am sure that neither death nor life, nor angels nor rulers, nor things present nor things to come, nor powers, nor height nor depth, nor anything else in all creation, will be able to separate us from the love of God in Christ Jesus our Lord.* (ROMANS 8:38–39)

All three episodes share a common theme. However varied and complex their motivations, Rodney, Alyssa, and James all sought relief and release *from* this world by striving after a higher, truer spiritual reality. In at least two of these cases, this spiritual escapism was masked by Christian themes and vocabulary. They pursued a perceived higher calling away from and above the matter and matters of created life. Some of their motivations are certainly understandable. We all can grow weary of this world, we sometimes need to escape for a while, and the difficulties of life can weigh us down. Christian vocations, however, will always draw us back into the world—back down to earth, so to speak. As God's redeemed and beloved creatures, we embrace the world He has embraced and long for the day when He will finally make all things new.

THIS-WORLDLY CALLINGS

Discovering our callings in the this-worldly rather than the otherworldly brings a number of significant challenges to us, as sinful creatures of "the climb." In the first place, our earthly callings are often boring, sometimes messy, and occasionally even painful. It's usually easier to run away from them, seeking the higher spiritual things. The difficulty is that escaping doesn't usually help us in the end anyway. We can become easily self-righteous—"*I'm* doing the true things of God, and *you're* not." Often, we'll find just as much sin in the super-spiritual as in the mundane. This was Martin Luther's accusations against the monastic institutions of his day. What is more, our self-chosen spiritual callings are seldom truly useful. When we seek this-worldly callings, at least we know that, however imperfect, they benefit our fellow creatures.

God calls us back down to earth to live a grounded life. Along with some challenges, great blessings come from heeding this call. Most important, our callings are easily discoverable because they are right at hand. There is little need to seek, search, or strive to uncover these vocations. They remain as close and apparent as making breakfast cheerfully, studying diligently, working tirelessly, serving sacrificially, and worshiping faithfully. Indeed, it is precisely because these callings are present daily before us that we become easily dismissive of them and seek to supplant them with the super-spiritual. We know them too well and grow weary at our failure of them. The solution, however, is not to escape from them. Rather, it is to return to Christ, who fulfilled them all for us and, receiving His forgiveness, be renewed in the creaturely callings He gives us.

This leads to the most important blessing of discovering your calling in the mundane matters of God's world. It draws you closer to Jesus, who took on our true flesh and blood. In becoming fully a human being, He brought infinite value to God's finite creation. He thought, felt, lived, loved, and worked as we do, yet in perfect, contented obedience to the Father's will. Though our life on this earth remains marred by this constant climb to be what we are not and could never be, in Jesus we have grace in abundance and new life, to live life. We cannot draw closer to Christ by becoming more than human. But because He became fully human on our behalf, giving us His righteous life as a gift through Baptism, we can embrace who we are as God's beloved creatures, and the callings given to us in this place. Through faith in the incarnate Christ, we become much less than God, yet more fully human.

· ·

> The maker of man became Man, that He, Ruler of the stars, might be nourished at His mother's breast; that He, the Bread might be hungry; that He, the Fountain, might thirst; that He, the Light might sleep; that He, the Way, might be wearied by the journey; that He, the Truth, might be accused of false witness; that He, the Judge of the living and the dead, might be brought to trial by a mortal judge; that He, Justice, might be condemned by the unjust; that He, Discipline, might be scourged with whips; that He, the Vine, might be crowned with thorns; that He, the Foundation, might be suspended upon a cross; that Courage might be weakened; that Security might be wounded; that Life might die.[40]

· ·

Through faith in the resurrected Christ, we know that one day our full humanity will be restored, and we, together with all creation, will sing His praises eternally.

. . . .

40   St. Augustine, Sermon 191.1, in *The Fathers of the Church: A New Translation*, vol. 38 (*The Writings of St. Augustine*, vol. 17), trans. Mary Sarah Muldowney (New York: Fathers of the Church, Inc., 1959), 28. Trans. alt. The copyright for this volume has expired and has not been renewed.

For Discussion

1. "Our physical, social, and emotional selves are inseparable" (page 97). Give some examples from your own experience which confirm this.

2. How is describing the condition of sin as a climb helpful in understanding its scope and seriousness (pages 98–99)?

3. Why was the physical reality of the suffering and death of Jesus necessary for our salvation (pages 102–3)?

4. Why is the bodily resurrection of Christ so crucial for the Christian message (pages 103–5)?

5. What was so dangerous about the gnostic heresy (page 106)? Can you discern any gnostic tendencies in our modern world?

6. What are dangers of "spiritual escapism"? Give some real life examples you have encountered.

7. Why did Martin Luther so vehemently object to the practices of the sixteenth-century religious orders (page 109)?

8. "Christian life will not be an escape from creaturely life but a calling to it" (pages 109–10). Discuss.

9. How was Martin Luther's recovery of the true understanding of vocation beneficial for society (page 110)? Is it applicable today?

10. Rodney misunderstood what it means to be spiritual. What were the consequences of this confusion (page 112)?

11. What important insight about vocation did Alyssa discover (page 114)?

12. "God calls us back down to earth to live a grounded life" (page 118). What changes might this mean for your life?

CHAPTER 5

GOD-GIVEN

*Our calling in life is better understood as
God-given rather than self-chosen.*

Choices

Deciding on a college to attend is one of the biggest decisions a family makes. Lukas understood this, so when the barrage of emails from Midwest universities spammed his inbox, he actually took time to read them—well, at least *some* of them. Throughout his entire junior year, Lukas and his mom sorted his mail into boxes positioned near the front door of their house, one marked "review" and another "recycle." This helped keep their rather tidy living room in decent shape amid the almost daily flood of college recruitment materials arriving via snail mail. Choices. It can be overwhelming, especially for a conscientious young man like Lukas, who was always eager to please and seldom without a plan for the future.

First, there's the field of study. He has the brain power for engineering, but last summer's congregational mission trip piqued his interest in ministry. Then there's the university. Choice A has a wonderful location and a great Christian atmosphere but no engineering program. Choice B is a huge state school but not the best location.

---

41   In this and other chapters, I am grateful for the insights and discussions of Concordia University Chicago students during our January 2020 Spiritual Life retreat.

Choice C—that's where his mom and dad met and his older sister attended, but he isn't interested. Lukas wants to blaze his own path.

Two additional significant factors complicate the decision: his music and his girlfriend. Lukas isn't planning to go into music as a profession, but he's a first-chair trumpet and would love to play in a good college band. His girlfriend, Charlotte, wants to combine her interest in science with her love of people and go into nursing. Adding his girlfriend and his trumpet into the mix makes the right-fit college recipe really difficult to perfect. Lukas and Charlotte have the maturity to know that spending four years apart with occasional visits over breaks would strain any relationship. Charlotte also secretly worries about living under Lukas's shadow for another four years. She has talents, ambitions, and dreams of her own and doubts she can fully flourish at the same school as the man she loves. Can she become who she's meant to be while always being known as "Lukas's girl"? They're going to have to have some difficult conversations going forward. When one young person's dreams diverge from another's, their love might stretch to the breaking point.

Choices—they'll only expand during college life. Who will my new friends be? Should I switch from an employable major to one I love, and will my mom and dad be okay with the debt load if I do? When is it time to hang up the cleats, because I loved sports in high school but the university level is a whole new commitment?

The further along you get, the more anxiety-producing the choices become. They line up at your door, incessantly knocking like you owe them money: decisions about friends, major, profession, relationships, marriage. What if you make the wrong decision and the course of your life is forever altered? What if you miss that one great calling God has earmarked for you? Will He be angry? Will you be less fulfilled? Could it ruin your life and derail you from your divine purpose?

It's easy to become overwhelmed by the number and intensity of the personal decisions you have to make in life. Especially standing in Lukas and Charlotte's shoes, it feels like the entire trajectory of life might change dramatically contingent upon a singular choice. In their case, they fortunately had a number of excellent personal resources to help them through the anxiety. They both had good parents with valid opinions but the wisdom to refrain from micromanaging their seventeen-year-olds' life choices. They both came from strong Christian communities that promised to pray for them as they sought God's will for their lives. Their close-knit group of friends knew and loved them equally and promised to give them honest advice, even if they didn't want to hear it at times.

The best wisdom, however, came from the chaplain at their Christian high school. In what would be a powerfully relieving moment for Lukas, the chaplain counseled that, in reality, most of the callings we have in life, we don't choose for ourselves. God gives them to us. He reminded Lukas, "You're fixated on your own personal judgments and the enormity of where they might take you. What you'll find out, however, is that most of the important things you're asked to do, you had little choice in the matter." The chaplain went on to explain how unexpectedly our callings come into our lives. In his case, he never would have dreamed God would place him as a pastor at a high school. He had "bigger plans" at seventeen. Sometimes we're so caught up in the callings we choose that we forget how many we've already been given.

Charlotte also received some sage advice. The chaplain gave her permission to take a break from anxiety-producing decision-making, at least for a while. He advised that she should concentrate on things she could control and callings already given her before she worried too much about the future. Our present callings are plenty to worry about. "God will get you where you need to be in the end," the chaplain assured her, "and He will bless any decision made in faith and love."

The big lie of the one big choice afflicts young people the most. It's usually described in this way: "There's a single, spectacular, self-chosen calling out there for you on this earth, and it's your job to spiritually discover what it is and then go out and fulfill it." This puts enormous personal and spiritual pressure on people and can even distract them from the many present, ordinary relationships and responsibilities God has already given.

Think again about the faces, places, and spaces of your life (see chapter 1): the people you daily encounter; the settings of home, school, work, neighborhood, and planet; the offices you occupy or the roles you're given. How many arose from your own personal volition? In retrospect, very few indeed. *Most* of our callings we don't choose, and even the ones we do choose seldom turn out the way we expected.

You didn't choose your family. Parents certainly decide to have children, but they don't get to pick the individual daughters or sons they'll be asked to raise and love. God gives them. You don't get a vote on who your siblings are—as much as you might want to at times! God forms your family and calls you to love and serve them with diligence and grace. None of us was consulted about who our parents would be—or our grandparents, aunts, and uncles for that matter. Yet these are some of the most formative and lasting relationships we'll have in life. It's apparent how easily distracted we become with the few callings we actually do choose while neglecting many we don't. We obsess about making the right momentous decision, all the while forgetting the callings we've already been given: a baptized child of God, a fellow creature on God's beloved earth, a loving member of a family, a conscientious co-worker or colleague, a good neighbor or teammate, a faithful Christian.

This is certainly the case in what might be described as the less-than-nuclear family. No one goes into a marriage expecting a divorce; the consequences for family life are both real and regrettable. God the Holy Spirit, however, works to bring repentance, forgiveness, healing, renewal, and new life in families that did not go according to plan and are broken by sin. In other words—*all* families. Stepchildren and half-siblings especially may feel pain and disappointment. They rarely have any control over the changes they experience, which can lead to frustration, disillusionment, resentment, or anger. The truth is, however, while God does not will divorce, He does will that blended families regard these new relationships as callings. Stepchildren and half-siblings don't choose one another—but neither do any siblings! They can, however, choose to live lives of charity and grace toward one another, seeing their relationships as opportunities to exercise a sacred vocation in the family life they've been given. They can also learn to trust that God is also the God of Plan B. A less-than-nuclear family can become a more-than-wonderful example of faithfulness amid unexpected callings, showing Christ at work even amid human frailty.

Just like you don't choose your family, you also don't choose, for the most part, your classmates or co-workers. No doubt the atmosphere of a workplace or the educational culture of a school may affect your decision to apply, attend, and remain at a job or school. But you're ordinarily just placed with others with whom you'll study, work, and play. A fourth grader doesn't handpick her classmates. A college freshmen has no veto power over who's enrolled in first semester psychology with her. A solider doesn't advise Uncle Sam as to who'll be accompanying him to basic training. A teacher doesn't get to handpick who's employed at her school. It is certainly the case that we choose employment at a certain business or organization and a number of factors sway this decision: pay, skill level, opportunities for advancement, location, and work environment including fellow employees. But unless you're the CEO, HR director, or in a specific management role, you don't select your co-workers. Ultimately, you have to concede that God has placed these people in your life as a boss, supervisor, colleague, or fellow employee. Hopefully, many blessings will adorn these relationships, such as an enjoyable working environment, satisfying accomplishments, and lasting relationships. Unquestionably, you'll also experience disappointment and frustration, which is all the more exasperating when you feel more or less stuck with people.

But what if you began to view these relationships as God-given? How might it change your perspective to embrace these people as ones God has placed in your life for a reason and a season, whom you've been asked to serve and from whom you might need to receive His blessings?

Similarly, we don't normally choose our neighbors. Again, you might select a community in which to live or perhaps even intentionally reside near a friend or relative. But no one gets to review the condo community's residence list before moving in. You don't get to vote a fellow student off the dorm floor. Neighborhoods change, and the neighbors you had when you purchased your home may not be the ones living next to you when you sell it. Our culture is increasingly transient, and much of this is beyond our control. The reality is, most of our daily interactions—our fellow travelers on the train, our classmates or co-workers, our neighbors and fellow citizens, the members of our congregation, and even those of our own family— have been brought into our lives with little choice on our part. Each of these can be regarded as callings: people for whom Christ died whose lives have been woven into ours. It is precisely because most of the relationships we have are not of our own choosing that they are given divine significance.

For every man his neighbor is a moving reality to which God's command is joined, "Thou shalt love thy neighbor as thyself." Without his having any choice, his neighbor is given to him.[42]

Four Sacred Gifts of God-Given Callings

The people in your life, God placed there. The opportunities you've been given, God opened up for you. The talents and abilities born or bred in you, God gifted them to you. Even the crosses you bear and the challenges of life can be seen as coming from His hand. The vocations we have should be interpreted as God-given. Four sacred gifts

42   Wingren, *Luther on Vocation*, 203.

follow when, by the work of the Holy Spirit, we regard our vocations as coming from God's hand: *value, strength, grace,* and *joy.*

In the first place, those I encounter daily have *God-given value.* I cannot simply dismiss people God has brought into my life as inconvenient or insignificant, no matter who they are. My parents deserve honor and respect, even when I'm reluctant to give it to them. My siblings receive my love and friendship, even when we don't agree. The neighbor across the street who needs some extra help was brought to me by God. He is not just a happenstance or accident of fate or chance. My colleagues, co-workers, or classmates have value and meaning, even though I might find them occasionally tiresome. Since God has so directed our paths to cross, I cannot in negligence or callousness dismiss them from my life. God has brought them to me, and thus the calling I have to serve them is from Him.

Because many of our God-given callings are difficult, He also promises to give us *strength* in fulfilling them. If they were not from Him, no such promises would accompany them. But since they are from Him, we can be certain His strength will accompany us. God does not call us and then abandon us. He promises to uphold us in every calling, no matter how difficult it may be. Even when we grow weary and our burdens seem too heavy, we have the promise of God's presence amid the things He's given us.

> *Have you not known? Have you not heard? The LORD is the everlasting God, the Creator of the ends of the earth. He does not faint or grow weary; His understanding is unsearchable. He gives power to the faint, and to him who has no might He increases strength. Even youths shall faint and be weary, and young men shall fall exhausted; but they who wait for the LORD shall renew their strength; they shall mount up with wings like eagles; they shall run and not be weary; they shall walk and not faint.*
>
> (ISAIAH 40:28–31)

Along with strength, we receive His assurance of *grace* when we fail. If my callings are God-given and not self-chosen, the amount and intensity of my failures are certainly multiplied and amplified. When I neglect a relationship, fail to exercise charity in a difficult situation, or refuse to bear a cross given, I sin against the living God because He has placed these in my life. How often and greatly we sin then! Indeed, the more we grow in awareness of God's callings upon us, the more sin we will recognize. This is why a deeper awareness of the God-givenness of life must always be accompanied by an even deeper awareness of His grace. The forgiveness of our sins in Jesus Christ—His blood shed for us and His life lived on our behalf—remains the only source of eternal comfort as we strive to lead God-pleasing lives amid our God-given responsibilities. God's grace is promised to all who trust in Him, and this grace enables us to embrace fully what

He has given, knowing that when we do fail, His love will abound evermore.

> *But now the righteousness of God has been manifested apart from the law, although the Law and the Prophets bear witness to it—the righteousness of God through faith in Jesus Christ for all who believe. For there is no distinction: for all have sinned and fall short of the glory of God, and are justified by His grace as a gift, through the redemption that is in Christ Jesus, whom God put forward as a propitiation by His blood, to be received by faith.*
>
> (ROMANS 3:21–25)

Finally, seeing our callings as God-given also brings us *joy*. Every mouth we feed in His name, or act of sacrifice done for His sake, or persecution endured for Him, or menial task received as from His hand, brings a sense of satisfaction because they are done as *from* Him and ultimately *for* Him. Were our callings not from Him—if they simply arose from us—then no true joy could accompany them. But because God has given them for us to do—and indeed has empowered us to do them—then joy abounds in fulfilling them, knowing our heavenly Father has asked us to be faithful.

> *So if there is any encouragement in Christ, any comfort from love, any participation in the Spirit, any affection and sympathy, complete my joy by being of the same mind, having the same love, being in full accord and of one mind.*
>
> (PHILIPPIANS 2:1–2)

The Holy Cross in Holy Callings

The cross of Christ shines through each of the four sacred gifts of our God-given callings. First and foremost, human beings as individuals have value because Christ died for them, loves them, and has redeemed them. We all stand equally condemned under God's righteous Law, yet equally forgiven and redeemed by His grace. The cross is the lens through which I must interpret every human interaction and relationship.

Only in Jesus Christ are we one; only through Him are we bound together. He remains the one and only mediator throughout eternity.[43]

DIETRICH BONHOEFFER

God gives us crosses to bear; this also is a sacred calling because it's from Him. The cross of Jesus Christ is God's heartbeat of love for us. He promises to draw near to us, even when we feel frustrated

---

43   Bonhoeffer, *Life Together*, 33.

or weary in fulfilling what He has given. Because God comes to us in difficulty, as the cross makes so clear, we can trust His present strength for whatever is placed upon us.

> Be patient and await His leisure
>   In cheerful hope, with heart content
> To take whate'er thy Father's pleasure
>   And His discerning love hath sent,
> Nor doubt our inmost wants are known
> To Him who chose us for His own.
>
> Sing, pray, and keep His ways unswerving,
>   Perform thy duties faithfully,
> And trust His Word, though undeserving,
>   Thou yet shalt find it true for thee.
> God never yet forsook in need
> The soul that trusted Him indeed.
>
> *LSB* 750:3, 7

God's grace shines forth from the cross. No failure, shortcoming, or sinful stumbling can separate me from His love given in the cross of Jesus. Constant and abundant grace will be needed in the many callings He gives. None of them will ever be perfectly fulfilled in this life. Every relationship, activity, and responsibility remains tainted as we live outside the Garden of Eden and before the garden of eternal life. Because we see these as callings from God, we also must cling to His mercy and grace at the cross in our inevitable failure of them.

For the joy set before Him, Jesus endured the cross and its shame. The taking-up of our God-given callings similarly brings joy to the Christian. Our Lord Jesus joyfully undertook the hardest task at hand—carrying the cross and upon it the wicked weight of the sin of the world. His cross both inspires and empowers us to joyfully fulfill our callings because they are God-given and God-pleasing.

> *Therefore, since we are surrounded by so great a cloud of witnesses, let us also lay aside every weight, and sin which clings so closely, and let us run with endurance the race that is set before us, looking to Jesus, the founder and perfecter of our faith, who for the joy that was set before Him endured the cross, despising the shame, and is seated at the right hand of the throne of God.*
>
> (HEBREWS 12:1–2)

Four Sacred Stories

GOD-GIVEN VALUE

Anyone but him. Chelsea auditioned for the fall production of *Our Town*, not because she was a theater major but because she hoped to expand her social circles and keep busy and because she always had a flare for the dramatic anyway. It was a good choice, but when she found out that Cody also had auditioned and received a small part in the play, Chelsea nearly screamed. Annoyingly self-righteous, obnoxiously overconfident, ever the know-it-all, Cody was the absolute *last* person with whom she wanted to spend hours of late-night rehearsals. Plus, well . . . they had a history together. First semester freshman year they both got caught up in the excitement of meeting all these new, fresh faces in college. In that sense, their short-lived but disastrous relationship was understandable. Although it had ended by October, they made some big mistakes. Chelsea still shook her head and cringed when reminded of it. Some things you can never get back. Seeing his name on that cast list brought a wave of reminders and regrets for her. Anyone but *him*.

It took until tech week for the director to finally confront Chelsea. Everyone's nerves were frayed by week five of rehearsals. Chelsea hadn't been a good classmate, cast member, or sister in Christ to Cody. First she avoided him, then was short and snippy with him, then fully dismissive of him, belittling him offstage and behind his back. *Our Town* had become *Our Troubles*, starring Chelsea and Cody, and everyone had seen enough. Cody several times tried to talk with her privately, directly, and as maturely as possible. He even attempted to apologize for past wrongs, but Chelsea held on to regret and resentment like she wanted as much drama in life as on stage.

The director had to address it with her. "Mr. Puck" was their new, youthful theater professor (a reference to the Shakespearean character in *A Midsummer Night's Dream*; the director's first name was Robin, but no one called him that). Mr. Puck asked her to stay after rehearsal one evening and began with a simple question: "Chelsea, who's directing this show?"

"Well, you are, of course," she replied defensively.

"No, not *this* show. The *big* show." That got her attention. After a long pause, Mr. Puck went on to explain how sometimes God places us on stage with people we'd never choose for ourselves. "We can question His casting, and even His directing at times, but in the end you have to believe that He's pulled us together according to His wisdom and for His purposes. You don't get to choose the cast, but you can choose how you act."

Mr. Puck seldom outwardly expressed his faith, but when he did, it grabbed people's attention. After a long conversation, a few tears, and a short prayer, Chelsea came to realize what she'd been doing. She promised to address her unresolved issues with Cody privately and leave the drama for the stage. She learned a big lesson: as difficult as it was, she had a calling and responsibility even to Cody. She didn't have to get back together with him. She didn't even necessarily have to *like* him. But every member of that cast brought a God-given calling to bear on her life: those she liked and those she didn't; the principal characters and the assistant stage manager; the director and the understudy. If the cross of Jesus was for her, it was also for them. And if God gave her these callings, she'd have to trust that He would give her the grace and strength to fulfill them.

GOD-GIVEN STRENGTH

"Jenn and Jeff." Everyone loved the sound of that, but they loved the two of them together even more. Finally married in their mid-forties, both had struggled through young adulthood to find a good Christian spouse. After years of loneliness, Jenn had even given up on the idea of marriage when she finally met and fell in love with Jeff. God has a way of surprising us sometimes. It didn't take long for them to know they were right for each other. When your face hurts because you're smiling all the time, it's a pretty good sign.

The first three amazing years of marriage brought little doubt to their minds that God had brought them together. The vocation of husband and wife is easily seen as a gift from God amid the blessings of love, joy, companionship, and mutual support. Year four would change all that. After an unexpected tumor in Jeff's left lung, a grave diagnosis, and a long, difficult illness, Jenn's physical and emotional strength stretched in ways she never could have anticipated when she vowed "in sickness and in health . . ."

The end was not pretty. Jeff's body deteriorated more quickly than anticipated while the drugs made him either incoherent or irritable. No one could have faulted Jenn for giving up on Jeff or for asking the toughest questions of God: "After years of waiting and praying, is this what You had planned all along? Three happy years and then three months of pain? Is that the deal I get? I finally meet the man of my dreams and then get dragged into a nightmare with him?" Although she struggled with God in her honest moments, Jenn also cared patiently, tirelessly, and faithfully for Jeff—truly modeling the life of Christ for him and others.

> *Then He said, "Your name shall no longer be called Jacob, but Israel, for you have striven with God and with men, and have prevailed."*
>
> (GENESIS 32:28)

Jenn understandably had moments of struggle, but she refused to let go in her wrestling match with God until she received His blessing (Genesis 32:27–30). She did not choose this calling when she chose to marry Jeff. Though she would not ever be able to fully understand it, ultimately she came to believe that God had given this to them to bear together. The cross of Jesus meant that He would remain with them, even draw near to them in their sufferings. Christ would give Jenn strength to fulfill this most difficult but sacred of callings. There was much Jenn would never understand as she cared for her dying husband. But the experience taught her this much: if the calling comes from God, then the strength will come from Him also. Jenn never remarried, but the faith formed in her amid that fiery trial bore witness to many for the rest of her life.

No saint on earth lives life to self alone
Or dies alone, for we with Christ are one.
  So if we live, for Christ alone we live,
    And if we die, to Christ our dying give.
In living and in dying this confess:
We are the Lord's, safe in God's faithfulness.

For to this end our Lord by death was slain,
That to new life He might arise again.
  Through sorrow on to triumph Christ has led,
    And reigns o'er all: the living and the dead.
In living and in dying, Him we bless;
We are the Lord's, safe in God's faithfulness.[44]

LSB 747

God-Given Grace

Gary needed to talk to someone. It was time. He wasn't one to easily admit his mistakes, but the feeling of conviction had grown into guilt, and then to shame, and now almost to despair. He didn't know his pastor very well and, to be honest, hadn't felt very comfortable with him. Pastor Paul had been at the congregation for seven years, but still many regarded him as the new pastor. Gary remained close to Pastor Ehrhardt, who had confirmed him nearly twenty-five years ago, even though he had long since retired and was living in Florida near his grandkids.

Although his church attendance had waned during his young adult years, Gary recently reengaged with his congregation and his faith. The birth and Baptism of a beautiful baby girl will do that for you. Pastor Paul welcomed this change in him and eagerly met him for midafternoon coffee even though it was technically the pastor's

---

44   Hymn text: © 1997 Norman J. Kansfield. All rights reserved. Used by permission.

day off. Uncomfortable at first, Gary began to open up. He had to because the guilt had become overwhelming. The problem centered on the many ways Gary believed he had failed God in his life. Almost neurotically analytical, the new father couldn't stop thinking of the sin saturating his life. He started with the past. Two years at a state school known for partying wasn't the best choice, in retrospect. Gary felt he wasted his parents' money and the natural intelligence with which God had blessed him. He eventually finished his degree, moved back home, and transferred to a local trade school, but he would never get back the time and talent he had squandered.

Next, there was the relationship he had prior to meeting his wife. Against his parents' wishes and his better judgment, he and his first serious girlfriend lived together for two years before Gary ended it. The worst part of it was that Gary knew he had been using her for the last six months of their relationship. She wasn't a Christian, and he even used that as an excuse to break it off with her. The hypocrisy and insincerity of his thoughts and actions during that dark time convicted him deeply.

His current situation brought him little relief from the guilt. He shows up late to work but claims the full amount of hours. He's curt with his wife, even though she's one of the most amazing women he knows. He doesn't pick up when his mom calls. And he's a poor example to his family, staying out late drinking on Saturday and then claiming to be too sick to get up for church. All this Gary poured out to Pastor Paul over a cup of coffee, while holding back embarrassing tears in a public place.

The pastor knew where to start. It would be a tough few moments, but he had to first affirm what Gary already knew. Gary had failed, and there was no way of getting to grace without an honest recognition of sin. Here's how Pastor Paul put it:

> Gary, I've got to tell you, you're right to feel this guilt. God has blessed you in incredible ways throughout your life, but you haven't seen His abundant blessings— or at least you haven't acted like you have. God gifted

you with relationships and opportunities that most of the world could only dream of having, but you haven't acknowledged that they're from Him. You *have* failed in so many of your God-given vocations, and it's worse because you know they're from His hand.

Pastor Paul paused and let that sink in. Perhaps surprisingly, Gary didn't get angry or make excuses. It was almost a relief to have someone acknowledge what his conscience and God's Word were already telling him. He *had* sinned.

What happened next truly brought relief, however. Pastor Paul forgave him his sins in Jesus' name. Right there, in that coffee shop, he placed his hand on Gary's head and pronounced absolution. It was a little informal and perhaps a bit awkward done in public, but neither of them cared at that point. The message couldn't have been any clearer. Pastor Paul delivered Jesus to Gary, reminding him of the power of Christ's cleansing blood, conveying the riches of God's grace to him, praying with him, and promising to keep close to him in the coming weeks and months as he tried to make important changes in his life.

Gary would continue to fail, as do we all so long as we remain on this earth. But he wouldn't forget that powerful moment and could live now in peace through his continued struggles. God's assurance of sacred grace will always be greater than our sin. Our responsibilities and obligations in our God-given callings are abundant, but His grace abounds all the more. No one can possibly learn of the God-givenness of their many vocations without also fully resting in God-given grace.

> *In Him we have redemption through His blood,*
> *the forgiveness of our trespasses, according to*
> *the riches of His grace, which He lavished upon*
> *us, in all wisdom and insight making known to*
> *us the mystery of His will, according to His pur-*
> *pose, which He set forth in Christ as a plan for*
> *the fullness of time, to unite all things in Him,*
> *things in heaven and things on earth.*
>
> (EPHESIANS 1:7–10)

GOD-GIVEN JOY

Twenty-five years of marriage, three beautiful children, a life of service to their community and their church: many considered Natalie and Micah the pinnacle of Christian witness. In particular, the couple approached every activity, obstacle, and relationship with a joyful attitude. They brought energy and excitement to the room. People looked forward to serving with them on yet another committee or initiative. As busy as they were, you wanted this dynamic duo on your side because you knew that the project would not just get completed but also that the work along the way would be enjoyable.

It hadn't always been this way. Their youngest son, Nathan, was born four years ago with special needs. This was tough on Natalie, in particular. Her whole life had been one of high goals, high performance, and high energy. She had never failed at anything. But Nathan seemed like a failure to her, although she would *never* say this out loud. Of course they considered him a "gift from God" (that's what his name literally means). Neither Natalie nor Micah ever bought in to the world's notion that a life is only worth living if it's fully productive. Still, she struggled with it, in her honest moments—what had she done wrong that this happened? Would she and Micah be able to bear this burden? How would it change their lives, and would they be resentful that Nathan would slow down their family and inhibit their ability to do all the things they felt God was calling them to do?

· ·

The elimination of the weak is the death of the community.[45] DIETRICH BONHOEFFER

· ·

Nathan's smile changed everything for her. That, and God's Word, of course. Nathan's joyful attitude toward everyone and everything coupled with his contagious fascination with the simplest things in life made him everyone's favorite. At first, Natalie and Micah hesitated to bring him to committee meetings or even to church. They weren't exactly embarrassed, but they didn't want their son, or their "burden," to distract or inconvenience people. Just the opposite was the case, however, as Nathan's winsome spirit lightened every room and every task. It didn't take long before people at church and in the community not only welcomed his presence at activities, they *insisted* on it. Of course, Nathan needed them—special energy and care were required for him to be integrated into the community. But *they* also needed *him* too. They needed his smile, his energy, his joyful presence, and the reminder that productivity and efficiency can't be the highest virtues of any organization.

Here's how Natalie describes the change that occurred within her:

> I had to get past the "how come?" and embrace the "what for?" That is, I couldn't exhaust any more energy contemplating why this had happened to my family and not another's, what I might have done to deserve this, or how a good God could allow these types of things to

45   Bonhoeffer, *Life Together*, 96.

occur at all. There would never be an easy resolution to these questions, and my fixation with them only distracted me from what I eventually came to see as an even better question, one I *could* find answers for: "In what ways could I see God at work *through* this?"

Nathan's smile reminded me that he wasn't worried about the origins of his condition. He was ready to accept God's purposes for it. Both Micah and I embraced Nathan and our new lives as a God-given calling, one that, like all others, would have both blessings and burdens accompanying it. But if it was from Him, we also knew that we could fulfill it with joy. Nathan was a "gift of God" to us in ways we never expected.

Joy accompanies those who see *their callings as God-given rather than self-chosen.* We're too easily distracted by the relatively few callings that we do choose, and thus become confused, angry, or disappointed when life throws us a curve ball. Some of the biggest questions about God's will, especially in times of suffering, will always remain. The greatest minds in theology and philosophy have never produced a neat and tidy answer as to the origin of evil, the "how come?" question. But the "what for?" is answered daily in a thousand ways by faithful followers of Jesus who receive joyfully all things as from His good and gracious hand. Their joy is sacred because it is from God, but also because it cannot be diminished by any circumstance in life.

Therefore, since we have been justified by faith, we have peace with God through our Lord Jesus Christ. Through Him we have also obtained access by faith into this grace in which we stand, and we rejoice in hope of the glory of God. Not only that, but we rejoice in our sufferings, knowing that suffering produces endurance, and endurance produces character, and character produces hope, and hope does not put us to shame, because God's love has been poured into our hearts through the Holy Spirit who has been given to us.

(ROMANS 5:1–5)

Blessings and Burdens

Because we interpret our callings as God-given rather than self-chosen, we know that whatever comes from them comes as from the Lord. And since we know the heart of God revealed in the work of Jesus Christ—His cross and life for us—we know that what God gives us will be good. Not necessarily fun, pleasant, or a walk down easy street, but good nonetheless. Since *He* is good, what He gives me to do is also good. This means that I must regard as blessings the particular things that come from my callings. Not things I have accomplished or earned or random benefits or the chances of fortune that have happened my way, but *blessings*—good things God has given despite my sinfulness and shortcomings.

Some of these blessings received in a God-given calling might be material. A talented lawyer is likely to be well-paid; live in an affluent community; have the best opportunities for her children in terms of schools, travel experiences, and extracurricular activities; and live in a stable community with abundant resources. But if this brilliant lawyer regards her position and material benefits as a blessing from a God-given calling, she lives a life of thankfulness and praise to God. She and her family sacrificially give back time, talents, and treasures to the church and community. They note well the advantages they've been given, pouring into those who haven't received the same, all the while seeking to be God's gloves in the lives of others (see chapter 3).

At the same time, the life of an accomplished lawyer will contain a number of difficulties too: long hours and late nights, tremendous stress dealing with complex legal issues, and court decisions valued in the millions of dollars. The job is accompanied by certain social pressures and responsibilities as well. Public, professional occupations come with expectations of behavior, intense scrutiny, the obligation to visibly give back to the community, not to mention time away from family and the health consequences of high-stress work.

There certainly are downsides to any occupation, but if you can understand your job as a calling from God, these burdens become bearable because He's the one who has placed them on you. Like the cross Jesus chose to bear out of love for us, we willingly and gladly accept the burdens of our various vocations, knowing that He who gives them to us also promises to strengthen us as we carry them.

Other blessings we receive might be related to the position or authority of one of our vocations. Parents, for example, call the shots, and their children owe them honor and respect under the Fourth Commandment. Christian parents are to exercise their authority in fear of God and out of love for their children, and indisputable blessings accompany their roles: the joys of establishing a family; you're never alone or bored with a house full of children; you direct and control the course of the day-to-day while also making the big decisions on behalf of the children; you're in charge of time, money, and resources. Regarding all of this as a good gift from God means that Christian parents employ these blessings in service to their children, while thanking, praising, serving, and obeying God.

All this He does only out of fatherly, divine goodness and mercy, without any merit or worthiness in me. For all this it is my duty to thank and praise, serve and obey Him.

SMALL CATECHISM, FIRST ARTICLE

Being a parent, however, also comes with burdens. Life is incredibly busy, and usually your personal needs sink to the bottom of the list. The health, wellness, security, and stability of your family falls on you. You're the last line of defense against the changes and chances of life. Your family has to come first, above your own needs and desires. This remains unquestionably hard. Any good parent will tell you it's probably one of the toughest things you'll ever do. But since fatherhood and motherhood are God-given callings, the burdens we bear in fulfilling them also come from God. This means that the burdens are *good*. God is at work through them in shaping us, disciplining us, and ultimately drawing us closer to Him. These are also, therefore, burdens we willingly and joyfully bear *because* they are from His hand.

Sometimes the blessings we receive amid our God-callings have to do with the particular relationships and human interactions of our work: good co-workers, classmates, or teammates; a dear friend on staff with you at school; members of a select team chosen for a special initiative who bring diligence and delight to the work at hand. Christians regard *people* as the best of God's blessings and recognize God's hand in bringing them into their daily lives. They didn't just happen to cross paths with you in a random coincidence with no deeper meaning or message. God brought them. God gave them. This means

He is to receive thanks and praise for them. It is likewise important for them to know that you regard them as a blessing from God.

I thank my God in all my remembrance of you, always in every prayer of mine for you all making my prayer with joy, because of your partnership in the gospel from the first day until now. And I am sure of this, that He who began a good work in you will bring it to completion at the day of Jesus Christ. It is right for me to feel this way about you all, because I hold you in my heart, for you are all partakers with me of grace, both in my imprisonment and in the defense and confirmation of the gospel. For God is my witness, how I yearn for you all with the affection of Christ Jesus. And it is my prayer that your love may abound more and more, with knowledge and all discernment, so that you may approve what is excellent, and so be pure and blameless for the day of Christ, filled with the fruit of righteousness that comes through Jesus Christ, to the glory and praise of God.

(PHILIPPIANS 1:3–11)

But people can also be burdens. We all know this. Some co-workers are cantankerous and unpleasant (we might be too at times!). Not all neighbors get along fabulously. You won't like all your teachers; and every teacher will have students that, well, they'd just rather not have. This is both theologically and practically inevitable: we're all sinners and we're all different. No organization, workplace, school, church, or family will be stress-free or conflict-free. Christians recognize this reality, remain self-reflective and repentant of their own shortcomings, and seek to receive the shortcomings and sins of others with grace. They also know that God shapes and molds their sanctified lives through the difficulty of dealing with the reality of sin in others. The promise of grace through His Word—both justifying and sanctifying grace—accompanies every burden given.

Finally, some blessings in our callings come from the tasks, activities, or context of fulfilling them. A state park ranger gets to work outside; a librarian where it's quiet. A college professor enjoys the academic life and three months free for writing and attending conferences. A pastor gets to use a variety of his gifts in service to the Gospel: social, academic, pedagogical, musical, and administrative. A welder works with his hands and can measure what he has accomplished at the end of the day. A research scientist uses her brain and reason to expand human knowledge, solve difficult problems, and make life easier for potentially millions of people. A mom might get to stay at home and experience the daily maturation of her children, with all the wonder and affection that brings. Whether it's family, labor, ministry, business, education, or finance, the particular context of our calling brings benefits. And while we certainly make decisions regarding the jobs we'll apply for and the lives we'll live, Christians also recognize God's blessed activity at work through it all.

Similarly, the type of tasks and the context of our callings will also surely bring burdens. A full-time mom has to put her career on hold. A bright, young, talented pastor probably could be making more money in a different field. A construction worker feels the toll on his body, and thus may have to retire earlier than others. A truck driver spends days away from his family in order to provide for them. A farmer's livelihood remains subject to external forces beyond his control, such as the fluctuations of weather, international markets, and government trade policies. A doctor may have to bring her patient the bad news of a chronic or terminal disease.

It's easy for us to covet the blessings of other people's vocations, but would we want their burdens too? When we interpret the burdens as God-given, we can come to regard them not with resentment or bitterness but as God's graceful work of drawing us to the cross to be strengthened and sustained by Him. The eyes of faith remain open to how God is at work in us for our good, even amid the challenges our present callings bring. Both the blessings and the burdens come from God.

STATIONS AND SEASONS

He loved the hectic life of being a young pastor at a growing congregation. Certainly, he stayed busy, especially with another calling to be a loving husband and father tugging at him. Pastor Kris's schedule never stopped. Once the busy day of ministry ended, another full schedule of babies, bath time, and bedtime awaited him at home. He wouldn't have it any other way, but the emotional and social energy required taxed his health and strength.

She was single, older, and had twenty years more experience in ministry than Kris. Margaret (everyone called her Miss Maggie) served Peace Lutheran part time as religion teacher in the day school, part time as music director, and part time as everyone's mom. No harder working, humbler, or more capable servant could be found in congregational life. Miss Maggie's ministry reflected the life of Jesus in sacrifice and love for those she served. She was also incredibly capable. The combination of talent and a servant's heart is a rare thing indeed.

Pastor Kris and Miss Maggie worked exceptionally well together. She was always welcomed at the parsonage, got along wonderfully with Pastor Kris's wife, and even got the privilege of being godmother to their youngest. They had their differences, of course. He could be rather scattered, catching the vision and seeing the big picture but not always following through on the details. Maggie loved details. They seemed to love her too, which is why she effortlessly collected them, stuck them on lists, and followed through on them with the cheerful efficiency of a hummingbird.

The secret of their shared success in ministry, other than the power of the Gospel, of course, stemmed from their ability to appreciate and respect both the blessings and burdens of each other's God-given callings. Kris knew that Maggie's single life burdened her. She had some dating experience in the past, but for a number of reasons—logistical and personal—nothing permanent had ever quite worked out. Miss Maggie was married to the church now. Her family flowed in and out of Peace Lutheran. This was certainly gratifying for her, but moments of regret, second-guessing, and insecurity occasionally surfaced. The holidays were always difficult for her, especially after the crescendo of worship and church activities gave way to the denouement of loneliness. The week after Christmas was the worst. Everyone had family to be with, the church building stayed quiet, and Maggie remained alone at her condo with a glass of wine and another novel to finish.

Maggie understood, on the other hand, Pastor Kris's high stress levels and near emotional exhaustion. Even this extroverted all-star grew weary of people. His biggest fear was leaving his wife and kids with the "Pastor Kris leftovers"—low energy at home, a short fuse, and nothing left emotionally to give.

It would have been easy for Maggie and Kris to covet each other's stations and seasons in life. From Kris's perspective, Maggie got to invest all of herself in ministry, merging her life with the lives of those she served. She got quiet time, study time, alone time, and flexibility with her own schedule. From Maggie's point of view, Kris had a family, a place where he belonged, and someone to come home to every night. He didn't need to rely on other people's charity to be included in events and holidays. He had a prominent position, was known and loved by many, and got to enjoy the life of a husband and father.

But Pastor Kris and Miss Maggie resisted the temptation to covet after each other's stations, praying for each other to regard their callings as from God. They both understood that God-given callings came with both blessings and burdens, things to rejoice in and crosses to carry. Being single and in ministry was lonely, but it also had freedom and opportunity. Being a busy pastor with a young family was taxing, but it also brought tremendous love, joy, and support. Miss Maggie and Pastor Kris modeled for the people they served an attitude of sanctified acceptance and appreciation for the present callings God had given while also supporting and encouraging each other in their different vocations. Most important, they respected and accepted each other as from God, rejoicing in blessings and bearing burdens together.

THROUGH THE WATERS

When Maria decided to go into nursing, she had no idea where that would lead. Two passions drove her through the late-night studies and the huge college debt: she loved helping people and she loved the gift of the human body. From her earliest memories, the beauty and complexity of God's greatest achievement—human beings—fascinated Maria. How we move, the miracle of the senses, and the creativity of the mind filled her with wonder and praise. Maria also had a soft heart. As a little girl with her neighborhood friends, she would set up a little doll hospital to care for patients. Maria, of course, was the nurse in charge of the living room ER.

Then, a particularly challenging and exhausting day at the hospital closed with her nearly in tears. Sitting on the train on the evening commute, she soberly reflected on both her past and current situation. Maria served as the director of nursing at a prominent hospital in the city. Instead of caring for patients, her days now were filled with spreadsheets, HR reports, state inspections, and insurance forms. Her role certainly came with many benefits: a nice salary, administrative responsibilities, and the ability to make real change at an institutional level. Days like today, however, caused her to second-guess herself and her calling. Had she lost sight of why she went into nursing to begin with? It was supposed to be about loving people and helping God's hurting creation, not about firing incompetent workers and fighting for insurance repayments. This might have been her lowest moment since becoming a nurse.

Feeling deflated, she opened the short devotional booklet she read nightly on the train. The reading assigned from Isaiah 43 seemed to match her situation perfectly:

> But now thus says the LORD, He who created you, O Jacob, He who formed you, O Israel: "Fear not, for I have redeemed you; I have called you by name, you are Mine. When you pass through the waters, I will be with you; and through the rivers, they shall not overwhelm you; when you walk through fire you shall not be burned, and the flame shall not consume you. For I am the LORD your God, the Holy One of Israel, your Savior." (ISAIAH 43:1–3)

Maria understood enough Bible history to know Isaiah's words referenced the children of Israel. She also understood that God's promise to them was like His promise to her, as a baptized child of the new covenant. Our callings in life will be difficult. We cannot always predict their path or measure fully their weight upon us. Although she wasn't facing *literal* flame or water threatening her life, the responsibilities of directing people and resources in the care of hundreds of patients and their families felt like it sometimes. So much depended on her. This was exciting, of course, but also hard. Knowing that God would be with her, through Jesus' promise, brought great comfort. Interpreting her present vocation as from God meant that she could acknowledge Him in the joys and satisfactions while also resting on Him when the waters overwhelmed her. Her lowest point also brought her closest to God's Word. Here's what she prayed that evening on the train:

Lord Jesus, I know that You have called my name in Baptism, redeemed me from all my sin, and sealed me for an eternity with You. Help me now also in the many callings of my earthly walk. Especially Lord, may I receive both the blessings and the burdens with equal joy, knowing that they come from Your loving hand. Strengthen me in the many tasks at hand. Be present through me for others. Bless me with an awareness of Your goodness to me. In Jesus' name. Amen.

SANS EVERYTHING

Shakespeare's famous quote about "second childishness" came to mind for him that rainy evening at the nursing home. It's from *As You Like It*, which Dr. John taught countless times to freshmen during his thirty years as an English professor. The words concluding the iconic "All the world's a stage" soliloquy resonated more than he wanted as he sat next to his aged father's bed by the window: "Sans teeth, sans eyes, sans taste, sans everything" (II, viii). Hooked up to an IV and wearing adult diapers, Dr. John's father was in rough shape, the end not far off. This once energetic, strong, and exceptionally talented dad seemed a shell of the man he used to be. He needed help doing everything, even just the basics for human survival. The Shakespeare quote came to mind because Dr. John now found himself caring for his beloved father like his father had cared for him as a child. As his dad once fed him, changed his diapers, entertained him, prayed with him, protected and advocated for him, John did for his father now. The poetic reversal that Shakespeare noted wasn't lost on this lifelong literature teacher.

The spiritual reversal wasn't lost on him either, which is what really mattered. Dr. John understood that he had been incredibly blessed as a son. Things were certainly not perfect: moments and even months of tension littered their shared journey like trash along the highway. After Dr. John's mom died, however, he and his dad came to an uneasy but lasting reconciliation. Now, it was John's turn. He would fill the role of a parent while his dad relied on him for nearly everything.

Resentment could have filled John's heart, as could jealousy of his siblings who lived across the country and thus couldn't be hands-on help. Regret and its companion guilt also occasionally worked their way into his sleepless nights during this trying time. But Dr. John made a different choice. He decided to accept these last and most difficult months with his dad as a calling, and arguably the highest calling a son can have. Burden though it be, if it came from God it came with a promise of grace and strength. Dr. John's dad would, in the end, lose everything as all of us will. But "sans everything" would not be the last line written about him. John knew that the heavenly Father who gave him this earthly father would bring them both together in eternity, where God would make all things new. *All* things. This faith gave Dr. John the strength to carry this burden as from God and the knowledge that, by carrying it, God was also at work drawing him closer to the cross.

That rainy evening, the room of a reconciled father and son brightened with the words of a familiar hymn, sung by a son who knew both the burdens and blessings of a sacred calling.

> In suffering be Thy love my peace,
>   In weakness be Thy love my pow'r;
> And when the storms of life shall cease,
>   O Jesus, in that final hour,
> Be Thou my rod and staff and guide,
> And draw me safely to Thy side!
>
> *LSB* 683:4

For Discussion

1. What advice would you have given Lukas and Charlotte? Would you have found the chaplain's words helpful (page 125)?

2. How might it change your attitude to see your co-workers or classmates as God-given (page 127)?

3. Regarding our callings as God-given brings four gifts. What are they and why are they important (page 129)?

4. What was the tough lesson Chelsea had to learn in their production of *Our Town* (pages 134–36)?

5. Jenn undoubtedly had to fulfill one of the hardest callings—caring for a dying loved one (pages 136–37). Share a time when you feel you had been given a difficult calling from God. What helped you fulfill this calling faithfully?

6. How had Gary failed in his various callings? What was effective about the pastor's approach with him (pages 138–40)?

7. Why was Nathan an unexpected gift of God for his parents? What did Natalie need to get past in order to fully regard her son as "God-given" (pages 141–43)?

8. Make a list of three blessings and three burdens you are experiencing in your current vocations. Discuss this list with a trusted friend.

9. Who are some of the people in your life that you consider to be your greatest blessings (pages 146–48)?

10. How did Pastor Kris and Miss Maggie effectively manage serving in church work together while also being in two completely different situations in life (pages 149–51)?

11. Maria drew great comfort from Isaiah 43:1–3 (page 152). How is this passage comforting for you?

12. How did Dr. John's actions and attitudes show that he accepted the care for his dying father as a God-given calling (page 154)?

BIBLIOGRAPHY

Atkinson, James, ed. *Luther's Works*. Vol. 44. Philadelphia: Fortress Press, 1966.

Augustine, Aurelius. Sermon 191.1. In *St. Augustine: Sermons for Christmas and Epiphany*, edited by Johannes Quasten and Joseph C. Plumpe. Washington, DC: Catholic University Press, 1952.

Bonhoeffer, Dietrich. Dietrich Bonhoeffer Works vol. 5, Life Together and Prayer Book of the Bible Edited by Geffrey B. Kelly. Minneapolis: Fortress Press, 2005.

Bonner, Gerald. *St. Augustine of Hippo: Life and Controversies*. 3rd edition. Norwich: Canterbury Press, 2002.

Brandt, Walther I., ed. *Luther's Works*. Vol. 45. Philadelphia: Muhlenberg Press, 1962.

Brooks, David. *The Road to Character*. New York: Random House, 2015.

BusinessWire. "Camping Is Up in the U.S., Trend Expected to Continue as Millennials Seek the Positive Health Impacts of Time Spent Outdoors." Accessed January 10, 2020. https://www.businesswire.com/news/home/20170315005391/en/Camping-U.S.-Trend-Expected-Continue-Millennials-Seek.

Concordia: The Lutheran Confessions. Second edition. St. Louis: Concordia Publishing House, 2006.

Forell, George W. *Faith Active in Love*. Minneapolis: Augsburg, 1964.

Grimm, Harold J., ed. *Luther's Works*. Vol. 31. Philadelphia: Muhlenberg Press, 1957.

Hendel, Kurt K. "Vocation: A Lutheran Understanding." Unpublished essay, used by permission.

Jodock, Darrell. "Gudina Tumsa awarded the Christus Lux Mundi." *Story Magazine* (Third Quarter: 2004), Luther Seminary, St. Paul.

Kolb, Robert. "Called to Milk Cows and Govern Kingdoms: Martin Luther's Teaching on the Christian's Vocations." *Concordia Journal* (Spring 2013).

Kolb, Robert. *Speaking the Gospel Today: A Theology for Evangelism*. St. Louis: Concordia Publishing House, 1984.

Kolden, Marc. *Christian's Calling in the World*. St. Paul: Centered Life, 2002.

Kolden, Marc. "Luther on Vocation," *Word & World* 3/4 (1983): 387.

Lenker, John, ed. *The Precious and Sacred Writings of Martin Luther*. Vol. 10. Minneapolis: Lutherans in All Lands Co., 1905.

Lutheran Service Book. St. Louis: Concordia Publishing House, 2006.

Lutheran Service Book: Agenda. St. Louis: Concordia Publishing House, 2006.

Luther's Small Catechism with Explanation. St. Louis: Concordia Publishing House, 2017.

Metaxas, Eric. *Bonhoeffer: Pastor, Martyr, Prophet, Spy.* Nashville: Thomas Nelson, 2010.

Pastoral Care Companion. St. Louis: Concordia Publishing House, 2007.

PBS NewsHour. "WATCH: Meghan McCain's Complete Eulogy for Her Father, John McCain." Accessed November 2, 2019. https://youtu.be/gymd1CScQ88.

Pelikan, Jaroslav, ed. *Luther's Works.* Vol. 3. St. Louis: Concordia Publishing House, 1961.

Ramirez, Richard. Unpublished homily preached in the Chapel of Our Lord, Concordia University Chicago. December 9, 2019.

The Commission on Theology and Church Relations. *Together with All Creatures: Caring for God's Living Earth.* St. Louis: The Lutheran Church—Missouri Synod, 2010.

Tumsa, Gudina. *Witness and Discipleship: Leadership of the Church in Multi-Ethnic Ethiopia in a Time of Revolution.* Addis Ababa, Ethiopia: Gudina Tumsa Foundation, 2003.

Veith, Gene Edward, Jr. *God at Work.* Wheaton, IL: Crossway Books, 2002.

Walker, Morton. *The Power of Color.* New York: Avery, 1990.

Weerts, Christine S. "St. Rosa Young." *Lutheran Forum* 43, no. 2 (Summer 2009). Accessed December 19, 2019. https://www.lutheranforum.com/blog/st-rosa-young.

Wingren, Gustaf. *Luther on Vocation.* Evansville, IN: Ballast Press, 2004.

Young, Rosa J. *Light in the Dark Belt.* St. Louis: Concordia Publishing House, 1950.